From Shad

The Incredible Adventures of
Shadrack the Self-Talk Bear™

BOOK 1 — *The Story of Planet Excellence*

The first book in the Shadrack series begins on the planet Excellence, the home of Shadrack and the Self-Esteem Team, who fight to save their planet from the terrible Negatroids.

BOOK 2 — *The Incredibears on Planet Earth*

Shadrack and the Self-Esteem Team travel to planet Earth to save the children, and confront the Negatroids in a giant amusement park filled with thousands of terrified Earth kids.

BOOK 3 — *The Rise of the Great Bear*

Shadrack, unarmed and alone, is forced to face the evil Negatroids who want to destroy him, when help arrives in the form of a mysterious bear with amazing powers.

Powerful, positive messages for children of all ages, from the world's leading authority on Positive Self-Talk.

Shad Helmstetter, Ph.D., is the pioneering dean of self-talk. He is the best-selling author of more than twenty books for grownups. In the remarkable Shadrack the Self-Talk Bear series, Dr. Helmstetter brings his life-changing message of self-talk to children of all ages.

www.shadhelmstetter.com

Listen to special self-talk for kids and adults from Dr. Shad Helmstetter

Self-Talk for Kids

Featuring Shadrack the Bear

Self-Talk for Older Kids

Self-Talk for Adults

Stream the top self-talk audio programs direct to your listening device.

www.SelfTalkPlus.com

The Incredible Adventures of Shadrack the Self-Talk Bear

Book 2

The Incredibears on Planet Earth

Published by Park Avenue Press
362 Gulf Breeze Pkwy., #104
Gulf Breeze, FL 32561

© Copyright 2018 / Shad Helmstetter / All rights reserved
© Cover illustration by Shad Helmstetter

No portion of this book may be reproduced in any form, printed, digital, or otherwise, except for brief quotations in reviews, without written written permission from the author. For information, address Park Avenue Press, 362 Gulf Breeze Pkwy., #104, Gulf Breeze, FL, 32561

Helmstetter, Shad
The Incredible Adventures of Shadrack the Self-Talk Bear
Book 2
The Incredibears on Planet Earth

ISBN 978-0-9970861-2-6 *(Printed format)*
ISBN 978-0-9970861-3-3 *(Digital format)*

For more information:
www.shadhelmstetter.com

Prologue

The planet Excellence, located in the constellation Ursa Major, is populated by bears.

In the planet's distant past, Excellence had been called the planet *Average,* and as planets go, it was definitely average—or below average. The bears that lived there were wild bears, and they were always either fighting each other or foraging for food, living in the wild, unkept and dangerous forests of the planet. The planet Average was not a safe or happy place to live.

But then, a very unusual bear, the *Great Bear*, had come to Average and had changed all that. He had taught the bears how to become intelligent, civilized bears who no longer waged wars and fought each other. He taught them how to raise food, and how to make better places to live, and how to live in peace. He had changed the planet Average into the planet that it is today, the planet *Excellence*.

The Great Bear had also taught the bears how to defeat the terrible Negatroids, the dark, shadowy, ghost-like creatures that had ruled the planet Average for eons of time, and had kept the bears in ignorance. The Negatroids had been defeated, and banned from the planet, and had fled to hide in the dark, far-off places of the universe.

The story of Shadrack the Bear began when the Negatroids returned to the planet Excellence—this time to steal the spirits of all the kidbears and youngerbears that lived there. But in a remarkable battle of positive against negative, good against evil, positive had prevailed, and the bears had defeated the terrible Negatroids once again.

After their defeat, the Negatroids had left the planet Excellence, and had fled to an unknown place in the darkness of space.

Chapter One

After the Negatroids

Many days had passed since the great Negatroid attack on Planet Excellence. The terrible Negatroids had come from distant space to destroy the bears of Excellence by capturing the spirits of all of the kidbears and freezing them forever in the cold, dark Nozone layer, high above the planet. But the Negatroids had been defeated by something so unusual that no one, except the bears of Excellence themselves, would have believed it could work.

But it did work, and the Negatroids were gone. The dark, shadowy, ghost-like creatures had left Excellence, heading for somewhere far off into space, and the bears of Excellence expected to never have to deal with a Negatroid again.

Now, for most of the bears, things had gotten almost back to normal. Shadrack and his best friend Wheely Bear could play *rolley* again with their other friends, and they no longer felt like they had to keep one eye on the sky above Excellence, watching for the darkness that had heralded the time when the terrible Negatroids had come.

Many of the bears of Excellence said that it was Shadrack who did the most to defeat the Negatroids, when he had ignited the skies of Excellence with the brilliant lights of celebration—exploding skyrockets of every color and description, with messages that filled the sky with "positive"—the one thing the Negatroids had feared most.

But Shadrack knew that it had been a team effort of all of the bears. The Negatroids, with all of their evil, negative ways, couldn't stand up to the positive spirit of the bears of Excellence.

Wise old Eli bear, however, who knew things about the future, had told the great council of elderbears that young Shadrack Bear was destined to become a leader of the bears of Excellence. And old Eli knew other things that even the elderbears could not yet know. Eli also knew that it would be necessary to prepare Shadrack for what was to come.

Much earlier, in the distant history of Excellence, when it had still been called the planet *Average*, there had been a bear who had been a great leader who had come to their planet.

That bear had led the bears who lived there, out of the dark, negative-thinking, war-like times of their past, a time of living in caves and fighting each other. That one, very unusual bear had led them to a bright, positive new future—the world of Excellence that the bears knew today. That, of course, was the bear known as the "Great Bear."

Because of the Great Bear, the bears of Excellence now had learning and education, real homes and schools, and the kind of positive goals and ideas that made their lives work. They even had sciencebears and technobears who had created wonderful starships (that were actually shaped like stars), so the bears of Excellence could travel to far-away planets.

The Great Bear had also given them his greatest teaching—the gift of "Self-Talk." Self-talk was the ability to turn bad into good, negatives into positives, and to see the future in a whole different way.

And he had also taught them how to use the art of *"Self-Talk for Self-Defense"* to get rid of negative thoughts and ideas, and create a planet of exceptionally smart and wonderful bears who learned to see life in the "positive"—and never in the "negative."

Learning the skill of using positive self-talk was important teaching for the bears of Excellence. Because of the teaching of the Great Bear, the planet Excellence had become the home of the most positive, forward-thinking, goal-setting, happy and productive beings in the whole universe. And in their world today, for most of the bears of Excellence, everything seemed just right.

Chapter Two

Bear Trust Forever

If there was ever a bear who wasn't afraid of anything, it was Shadrack Bear's friend, Wheely, the wheelchair bear.

"Wheely," as he was called by all of his friends, was distinguished by the fact that even though he had no feeling in his little bear legs or in his little bear feet and toes, and he couldn't walk or run, he had the ability to overcome *anything*.

Although he was like a small teddy bear who had no stuffing in his little legs or feet, that didn't stop Wheely Bear in any way. He could do more things with a wheelchair than most bears could do on their feet. Wheely could play every sport, and often win, and his attitude was amazing, and always positive. The lack of feeling in his little bear legs would never stop him.

Some nights Wheely would dream of actually being able to feel his feet, and wiggle his toes, like all his bear friends could. But even though in the daytime he could not be quite like the other bears, in every other way he was all bear. Wheely could move in his wheelchair faster than most bears could move on their feet, and he could do amazing things, like swivels and twists and turns at high speed, that all of the other bears of Excellence could only marvel at.

Wheely Bear was also Shadrack Bear's best friend. And he had been there when Shadrack and the bears of Excellence had defeated the terrible Negatroids, and driven them away from the planet Excellence.

Right now, Shadrack was talking to Wheely after a rolley tournament. It had been a good set of games, and both teams had won.

(Rolley is a game made up of two teams of eight players each, who throw a rolley ball down the length of the playing field toward the opposing end zone, and then use paddles and paws to return it. Randomly, throughout the game, an official shouts *"Rolley!"* and one team member from each team swaps sides—thus making it possible, by the end of the game, for every bear to end up playing for the other team.)

"I've been thinking, Wheely," Shadrack was saying. "If the Negatroids ever came back, or if we ever had to fight them again, I want you to promise me one thing."

"They're not coming back," Wheely said smiling, "thanks to you! You blew them away with good stuff! So now they don't like it here. Excellence is too *positive* for Negatroids. They *hate* positive bears and positive *any*thing."

As they talked, Wheely was doing small circles with his wheelchair, as he always did. Wheely maybe couldn't walk like other little bears, but that had never stopped him. He was one of the most active, always-positive bears on the entire planet.

"Okay, I agree they probably won't come back, but if it ever happened again, I want you to promise me something," Shadrack said. "I want you to promise me, *"Bear trust forever,"* that if Negatroids ever do come, you will signal me so I can help."

"I promise," said Wheely, backing his wheelchair up about six feet and then doing a high-speed figure-eight where the two of them were talking in the end zone of the rolley field. "I promise, I promise." And then he added, "but the Negatroids aren't coming back."

Wheely was very smart, and very good at thinking and understanding things, but he was especially good at maneuvering his wheelchair in the most amazing designs and motions.

"Good, then I have your bear trust promise?" Shadrack asked.

"You got it. *'Bear trust forever,'*" said Wheely, veering into a double 360-degree spin as the two of them left the rolley field.

As Shadrack and Wheely talked on that warm, sunny Excellence afternoon, at the end of a great day of rolley, neither of them could have known what was about to happen next.

* * * * * * * * * * *

For most of the bears of Excellence, things may have gotten back to normal, but not for old Eli Bear and the special team of technobears.

Eli was spending a lot of time in Science and Technology Cave, where he and the technobears were studying rows of instruments. Eli was searching for something. He was following the clues that were written in the old scroll the Great Bear had left for them.

The scroll had foretold the attack of the Negatroids. It had also said that the bears would be victorious, and that a new leaderbear would emerge. According to the scroll, that bear was named Shadrack, and he would help the other bears defeat the Negatroids when they attacked the planet Excellence. All of that had happened, exactly as the Great Bear's scroll had said it would.

"The Negatroids must be banished from this universe forever," the Great Bear had continued. The scroll had said that Shadrack would go on a long journey—and in the end, he would be called upon to save a great many children from a terrible enemy.

The scroll hadn't said exactly where that was, or who those children would be. But it was very clear who the "terrible enemy" was. It was the Negatroids. And right now, Eli was searching for them in the vast emptiness of space.

Chapter Three

The Planet Earth

Far away across the heavens, the small blue, green, and white planet called "Earth" turned its way through space as though it was the only planet of importance in the entire universe.

But on this little planet, things were not going so well. The species, called "humans," that ruled the planet, were having trouble keeping things on their planet under control. On Earth, instead of things usually getting better, things were often getting worse.

To begin with, although you couldn't hold it against them, humans looked *strange*, kind of like bears, in a way—but *without fur!* And they didn't act at all *civilized,* the way *bears* did.

Humans acted more like the way bears *used* to act. *Un*civilized. Always fighting, and hurting each other, and even killing other humans. They often acted like they were creatures from the far distant past who just happened to live in square little earth houses and buildings, instead of in caves or in the rocks or in trees.

And worst of all, these humans on planet Earth had the most absurd ideas. They thought *they* were the masters of the universe. (They didn't know that *bears* were the masters of the universe.)

Even though the humans had had their own great leaders in the past, they had forgotten most of what those leaders had taught them. So they spent a great deal of their time on Earth waging wars, or just fighting and squabbling, or being angry, or depressed, or just too busy, and always going nowhere important in a very big hurry.

On planet Earth there was too little thought given to things like how to be special, or how to be a quality person, or the importance of helping other humans. A lot of the humans who lived on Earth seemed to be too busy for that. And because many of them set goals to *buy* things—instead of setting goals to do incredible things with their *lives*—many of them weren't very happy at all.

Often, little humans, also called "kids" or "children," and even many of the grown-up humans, did not have enough to eat, or even a place to sleep. They were left to fend for themselves and were called "homeless," right in the middle of great cities with more homes than you could count!

There were good humans, of course. In fact, quite a lot of them. But they often seemed almost helpless to do anything much to change the way things had become on the once caring, beautiful planet called Earth.

Earth itself once had a different name from what it was now called. It was a name that was spelled with the same letters as Earth, but arranged differently. The planet Earth had once been called the planet "*Heart*."

Even now, if you took the last letter "h" from the planet's name "Earth," and put it back where it belonged, at the *front* of the planet's name, it once again becomes the word *Heart*. But these days, instead of living from their *heart*, almost everyone on Earth was busy living from the part of their brain that caused them to live in confusion or in fear.

Many humans were busy doing things that weren't really important at all, like watching negative news, or burying their noses in gossip and mindless chatter on their phones and on their high-tech tablets.

They were so busy doing these things that most of them would not even have noticed if sometime, when they were least expecting it, something very bad and very dark entered their skies, and came down into their lives and into their homes, and began to steal their children's spirits from them.

Which, of course, was exactly what was about to happen.

Chapter Four

The Arrival of the Negatroids

The shadowy, ghost-like form of the Negatroid leader *Low* looked toward his brother *No*, and both pairs of their slit-like eyes shined a harsh yellow-green of evil satisfaction. The two of them were observing something called "television" that was coming to them from the surface of the planet Earth, below them.

"Look at this!" Low exclaimed, concentrating on what he was watching on the control screen of the Negatroid warship *Neanderthal I*. "I never ever pray," Low said. "I don't even know *how* to pray. But if I did, this is *exactly* what I would pray for."

"What a perfect place to destroy completely," his Negatroid brother No hissed back at him. "*Humans!*" he almost shrieked out the word. "Look at them. They've almost destroyed *themselves!*" he croaked, barely able to conceal the fiendish joy he felt at finding such an amazing target for destruction.

"No species on any planet we have ever attacked has ever been so ready for us and our kind of *self*-destruction as these humans," Low wheezed, choking on his own ragged breath. "They are *perfect!*"

"I agree," No said. "They are *already* fighting. Probably always have been. They dislike anyone who is different. Half their population is clinically depressed, and the other half is self-medicating. A lot of them have problems with self-esteem and they already don't like themselves. They spend more time arguing politics than they do making peace. They can read and write, but look at what they're reading! Their books are gathering dust on shelves while they spend hours reading meaningless negative rants on their techno gadgets.

"Gangs of youths own many of their streets. Even young kids have learned to take drugs and drink things that put their heads into a vice. Their schools look like arsenals. The walls of their subways and buildings have our kind of words already spray-painted all over them. *What a target!* This place, this planet called Earth, is perfect for us! *Are you sure we haven't been here before?*"

"I think we just got lucky," Low chortled back. "The humans of Earth had it so good they forgot how to *keep* it. And now they're going to *lose* it," he wheezed.

"Want to see their little planet go all the way over the edge? Watch what happens when we start stealing their kids' *minds*. Watch what happens when their greatest hope—the spirits of their young ones—is taken away from them forever!

"*We will own the minds and the spirits of their children!*" the evil No screeched. "And there is nothing they can do to stop us!"

The dark gray mass of the Negatroid command ship *Neanderthal I,* with its armada of warships following behind like an evil cloud of darkness, droned its way through space high over the surface of the planet now called Earth, once the planet called *Heart,* above the white billowing clouds that still drifted through Earth's once brilliant blue sky. If the Negatroids had their say, it was a sky that, all too soon, would not be blue at all.

Chapter Five

Searching for the Negatroids

Back on planet Excellence, everything in Science and Technology Cave was in an uproar. "We've found them!" the technobear named Kim shouted.

"Are you sure it's them?" the sciencebear named Sazza asked, her bright bear eyes peering intently at the viewing screen that would show the bears of Excellence what they were searching for.

"Their spaceships look like the same dark gray armada we observed leaving Excellence," Kim Bear replied. "Same size, same mass, same negative, non-reflective albedo, same negative *everything*," he said. "It has to be them!"

"I'd better alert Eli," Sazza said, shaking her wise bear head sadly. "It looks like the Negatroids have found their next victims. What is the name of the planet you have them targeted on?"

"On our old charts, the planet was called "Heart," Kim Bear replied. "But something happened there. We don't know what, but something negative happened, and *Heart* became *Earth*," he said.

A short time later, old Eli arrived, and was soon studying the information that flowed across the screen in front of him as the science bears gathered around him.

"You are right," Eli said to Sazza. "The Negatroids could not have chosen a more vulnerable target. From what this shows us, Earth may not stand a chance against the Negatroids.

"The Great Bear often talked about the planet Heart," Eli went on, "and the great promise it held. The Great Bear told us that other than Excellence itself, the planet Heart was the most beautiful planet he had ever seen.

"As you remember, one time, a team of research bears from Excellence was sent to travel to a number of planets in that area of the galaxy, and Heart was one of them. But the research bears never returned, and all signals from them were lost. We waited many months for them to return, but they never did. The search vessel we sent to try to find them came back with nothing. And until now, that is the last we have heard of the planet."

After Eli had finished studying the information from far off in space, he asked Sazza to put on the screen any video of Earth they had been able to receive by scanning the Negatroid fleet for transmissions.

"We have been able to track and capture all of the video the Negatroids have picked up from monitoring planet Earth's visual transmissions," Sazza told him.

"On Earth, instead of holovision like we have here on Excellence, they call it "television." It's just flat, 2-D images, but the images are quite clear, so we should be able to get a good look at what the inhabitants of Earth are like. Would you like to see what we can bring up?" Sazza asked.

"Yes," answered Eli. "From space, the planet Earth still looks as beautiful as the Great Bear described it. Let's see what it looks like on its surface."

Within moments, scene after scene began to make its way across the large view screen. Old Eli and Sazza and all the technobears watched and listened intently, as life on Earth passed in front of them. Oceans, continents, cities, homes, automobiles, airplanes, animals . . . and humans . . . *millions* of humans.

As Eli watched Earth's television scenes, remembering the Great Bear's stories of the planet Heart, he suddenly became very, very sad. It no longer looked like the same planet the Great Bear had talked about. It had once shown such promise, but from what Eli and the other bears were seeing and hearing now, even that promise seemed in doubt.

If the Great Bear could see the humans of Earth as they were now, he, too, would have been saddened, Eli thought. Look what they've done with the beautiful planet they were given. And look at their *children*. Where are their parents leading them?

"What have they done?" he said sadly, almost to himself. When it was the planet Heart, they could do *anything!* But now, instead of living their dreams, they were losing them.

Chapter Six

The Vote

The olderbears who gathered in Great Hall were still talking in an uproar when old Eli entered and took his place at the front of the great room, surrounded on each side by the elderbears. The room abruptly fell into silence as Eli began to speak.

"Bears of Excellence," he said, "we have a challenge that requires your greatest attention. And it may require our greatest effort.

"After the Negatroids left Excellence, we decided to track them, to make certain they had truly left our planet, and to find out where they would attack next—a planet that would suddenly be in grave danger, and could perhaps use our help. The bears of Excellence have learned how to defeat the Negatroids. But their next target may not be so well prepared.

"To learn where they were going next, our technobears created a Negatroid signal-follower that allowed us to not only find them, but with the 'Negatracker' we are also able to capture any communications they are monitoring.

"We were able to locate them near what we now believe is their destination—a small, extremely vulnerable planet called Earth.

"Once the Negatroids placed their armada in an orbit above Earth," Eli continued, "they began monitoring Earth's own communication signals. When they did that, the Negatroids were able to tune in to a primitive form of holovision called television. And when the Negatroids intercepted the television signals from Earth, our own signal-follower allowed us to observe the same communications the Negatroids were picking up.

"Please watch these transmissions from Earth," Eli said. "Pay special attention to the messages the people of Earth are programming into their young Earth kids' minds. When you see this," old Eli said sadly, "you will see what has gone wrong on Earth, and you will see, with the Negatroids preparing to attack them, what is sure to be the outcome. Here are some of the transmissions we have received."

All of the large attentive eyes of the bears followed Eli's gaze as he turned to look at the giant holovision screen in front of them in Great Hall.

The screen flickered to life, and there, in an odd, flat, Earth-like television picture, the bears in Great Hall saw their first pictures of planet Earth.

They saw scenes of cities overcrowded with humans, and strange vehicles called "automobiles" lined up for endless miles on endless freeways. Next, there was scene after scene of wars and violence, bombs exploding, buildings burning, and people running in the streets. Then there were scenes of riots in big cities, teenagers in prisons, and guns were everywhere. Little children fought other little children, and every school had bullies.

Parents of Earth kids, who didn't even know they were doing it, filled their children's minds with the constant belittling thoughts and notions of negative self-belief. Never realizing that with their own negative words of fear and self-doubt, they were programming their children to live lives of uncertainty and failure, instead of lives of confidence and positive growth. On and on, scene after scene, the bears saw the plight of Earth, and it was *heartbreaking.*

And just as sadly, even the planet Earth itself looked to be in bad shape and getting worse. As a grim reminder of how Earth once had been, there were scenes of once beautiful forests—now stripped and barren, rivers running with pollution, and air so dark and filled with smog it looked like the *Nozone.*

The *Nozone,* as every bear of Excellence had learned, was the dark layer of frozen souls that formed at the edge of space above any planet the Negatroids attacked. That was where the Negatroids sent the spirits of the children to sleep in coldness and darkness throughout eternity. Every little spirit the Negatroids stole was sent to the *Nozone*. It was the place that the terrible Negatroids, unless they were stopped, would soon send the spirits of the children of Earth.

The olderbears of Excellence had seen enough. The message was all too clear. Earth was in trouble. And the Negatroids hadn't even gotten *started* yet. Just imagine what would happen to the kids of Earth when they did.

Eli next asked the elderbears to vote on what he felt must be done—that was: *"To send a team of bears to help save the children of planet Earth."* When the vote was taken, all of the bears assembled in Great Hall raised their paws skyward. The vote was unanimous.

With the vote taken, it was official. A team of bears from the planet Excellence would go to planet Earth to help the humans defend themselves against the terrible Negatroids.

Perhaps, just possibly, they could change the future picture of Earth itself, and help the planet Earth become the planet *"Heart"* once again.

Chapter Seven

The Mission

Wise old Eli Bear had already known which bear he would select to lead the team of bears who would be sent to Earth. And his first choice was the right choice. The old scroll from the Great Bear had foretold it, and now it was happening.

"Shadrack," Eli said, looking at the strong, positive, youngerbear who now stood before him. "Do you know why I have called you?"

"No Sir, I don't," Shadrack responded. "But it must be important."

"It is important," Eli said. "We were successful in tracking the Negatroids after they left Excellence, and we know where they are." And then he continued, "Watch these scenes from a planet the Negatroids have now surrounded, a planet called Earth, and you'll see what we have learned."

Shadrack watched the many scenes of planet Earth, and its people, and especially its children. There were scenes that showed the young humans winning and doing well. They had so much *potential* to do *good*.

But there were so many *more* of the *other* scenes—the ones that showed children and young people of Earth fighting and angry, troubled and confused, many of them headed for lives of worthlessness and failure instead of promise and achievement.

Life, for many Earth kids, was already chaotic—and spinning more and more out of control every day. Most of them had not learned how to be *positive,* and how *not* to be *negative*.

And they certainly were not at all prepared to defend themselves against the attack of the Negatroids that was about to begin. As Shadrack could see, things on Earth looked pretty grim.

When the view screen in front of them finally stopped on a final image of Earth, now surrounded by a frightening veil of Negatroid darkness, Shadrack, with a nod of complete understanding, turned to face Eli.

"I got it," Shadrack said. "I see what's happening. The Negatroids are going to destroy Earth's children and take their spirits from them," he said, his gaze strong, but shaking his head slowly, knowing too well what that meant for the children of Earth.

"Yes, Shadrack," Eli answered. "Unless something is done, that's *exactly* what the Negatroids are going to do."

Shadrack then paused, choosing his words carefully, and asked, "Why did you show this to me, sir? What can I do to help?"

"I have an important commission for you, Shadrack. I want you to go there," Eli said, nodding toward the image of the darkened Earth on the view screen, "to that far away planet that is in peril. I want you to put together a team of the most *positive bears* on Excellence—a team of bears who know how to *defeat* the Negatroids—and help save the children of planet Earth."

* * * * * * * * * * *

On the dark, ghostly command ship *Neanderthal I,* now poised in space above the planet Earth, the two Negatroid leaders were planning their first attack on the unsuspecting planet.

"Even before we strike, we are already winning," the evil Negatroid Low said. Every child of Earth we hit is a waiting target."

"How can we miss?" his equally evil brother No coughed back at him. "The kids of Earth are already so confused, so ready to fight and argue for no reason at all, and so used to all the negatives all around them every day—it will easy for us to defeat any simple idea of "good" they possibly have, and defeat them with an overwhelming mindset of *bad*.

"We will destroy the children of Earth with a three-phase attack," the evil Low said.

"First, *'Phase I.'* We will start with negative guerrilla warfare, with completely unexpected Negatroid sniper attacks, like the terrorists who already live there, but we'll be hitting random *kids,* from out of nowhere.

We'll hit them with negative, dark thoughts in their schools and in their homes, and on their playgrounds, and on their television sets, and on their phones and tablets, and in their video games.

We'll take out any good thoughts they have left, and fill their brains with negative! We'll finish what their careless elders have already started. And they'll never know it's us!

"Then comes *'Phase II,'*" the evil Low continued, his breathing ragged with excitement. "When the self-belief and self-esteem of the little Earth kids is crippled beyond repair, we'll find the biggest crowd of kids we can find, *all together in one place*, and we'll destroy *all of them*. Imagine, thousands of Earth kids, all together, losing *all of their spirits at once!*

"That will create a *panic* that will spread worldwide," Low said, his voice rising to a fevered, croaking pitch and his evil, yellow-green eyes glazed over as he spoke, "and when the Earth parents are panicking and scared to death of a pandemic of soulless, lost little kids, we'll finish them off with *'Phase III.'* We'll hit the *entire planet*, city after city, with *'The Giant Voice of Doom,'* and fill what's left of their minds with nothing but fear and despair!"

"They'll never know what hit them," his evil brother No agreed. "They're halfway there already! So many of the Earth people are already so much like us, saying *terrible, negative, bad,* and *harmful* things to their own

Earth kids. They won't even know we're helping them finish what they've already started—*destroying the minds and spirits of their little ones.*

"This is so much *fun*," No said, trying to rub his claw-like hands together in evil glee. And then, starting to dance a victorious dance of Negatroid joy, but forgetting he had no feet and couldn't dance, he ended up careening off the instrument panel, and after twirling, completely out of control in the air for an embarrassing five or six seconds, he ended up hanging somewhat upside down in the middle of the control room, trying to regain some sense of upright balance, looking clumsy and foolish as he did so.

Pretending he had spun out on purpose, No tried to hide a dark blush of embarrassment and said, "I *tried* to do that."

And then, finally getting his bearings once again, he said, regaining a bluster of confidence, "Are you ready, children of Earth?"

The evil No's ungainly mid-air spin may have made him look like a clumsy fool, but No and Low had the same dark look of determination on their shadowy faces. And No's final words were deadly serious.

"Ready or not, here we come!"

Chapter Eight

The Self-Esteem Team

It was early morning on the planet Excellence. Shadrack looked up at the beautiful sky above him. This morning the sky was aqua blue, with a touch of crimson and pink that announced the sun was about to rise.

As he looked at the sky, seeing how beautiful and clear it was, Shadrack felt thankful that there were no dark clouds of Negatroid war ships, and no cold gray Nozone layer darkening the skies of Excellence. His beautiful planet was *safe*.

But then, he immediately thought about the Negatroids spreading their darkness of negativity over *another* planet—a distant world that he would soon be traveling to, to help defend that planet from the evil ones who had come to steal its children's souls.

Eli had asked Shadrack to meet with him in the control center of Science and Technology Cave, and he soon made his way there and found Eli waiting for him.

"Before we begin," Eli said," there is something very important I must tell you; something you must keep with you and never forget." Eli waved one bear paw outward toward the huge technoroom they were seated in.

"All of this technology you see around you here, all of the technotools our bears of Excellence can make for you to take with you to Earth, things that will help you fight the Negatroids—all of those things are just that—*tools*, and nothing more.

"Your mission to planet Earth, Shadrack, will not be about the tools you take with you; it will be about the *heart* you take with you. When you fight the evil ways of the Negatroids, you must always fight it with *positive*, with *good*, just as you did when the Negatroids attacked us here.

"The Negatroids on Earth," Eli continued, "will expect you to lose your *heart* and your *belief*, in the end. But if you keep your heart, your quality of character, and never stop *believing in yourself*, the Negatroids will *never* defeat you."

Shadrack understood what Eli was saying, and he knew how important it was.

"I promise to keep my heart, I promise to always be positive, and I promise to *never* stop believing in myself, no matter how bad the Negatroids get," Shadrack said. And then he smiled a Shadrack smile, nodded his head and said, *"Bear trust forever."*

"Good," said Eli. "Then let's get started. Do you have your list of the team members you have selected to take with you to planet Earth?"

"I have written them down for you, sir," Shadrack said, handing the important list of names to Eli.

"I know you have carefully thought through each of your choices," Eli said as he read through the names. "Tell me why you chose each of these bears to go with you on the mission to Earth."

The list was titled, *"The Self-Esteem Team,"* and it was Shadrack's personal first choices of the bears of Excellence he had chosen to travel with him to planet Earth.

He began by saying, "I didn't list their names in order of importance to the team. Every bear on the list is important. That's what a team is all about."

Then, introducing his choices, Shadrack read aloud each of the names of the bears he had selected, and after each of their names, he added a few, important comments about each of them:

Wheely Bear (Wheelchair Bear)
"I choose Wheely Bear," Shadrack said, "because not only is he my best friend, but he is the most resilient bear I know. Wheely never quits, and he never gives in. He also knows what it means to overcome anything. Anything at all. And I would trust him with my life. So I choose him. And the fact that he is in a wheelchair never stops or holds him back. Wheely learned how to turn an adversity into an asset," Shadrack said, "something everyone should learn to do.

"Oh, and one other thing: when Wheely gives the *'Bear trust forever'* oath to a friend, he means it. *Forever.*"

Holly Bear

"Next, I chose Holly Bear. She's my sisterbear, and she is totally into great positive bear ideas. But I also chose Holly because she is smarter than any bear I know, not only in a school kind of way, but also in an *intuition* kind of way. She senses stuff. She just *knows* things. It's always smart to surround yourself with people who are smarter than you. Especially someone who has radar."

Believer Bear

"I chose Believer Bear to go with us because he can be anyone he wants to be. He's like a lot of bears in one. We could use an 'actor bear' when we go to Earth, because who knows what we'll get into? He can be, in his mind, an astronaut bear, a doctor bear, a farmer bear, or a wild bear. He can be anything. Believer has an amazing imagination. And sometimes, when things go wrong, what you need to have *most*, is *imagination*. Believer Bear has a lot of that."

Poppy Bear

"Poppy Bear will also be important for the team," Shadrack said. "Poppy motivates and inspires everyone. I know she has a sadness inside of her, because she lost her fatherbear, but she doesn't let it stop her. She has more energy and enthusiasm than any two other bears, and she's a natural cheerleaderbear. She understands how to keep having faith even when it seems like there is no chance of things working out. Knowing how *down* the Negatroids are, we're going to need to keep ourselves *up!*"

Theo Bear

"Next is Theo Bear. I know that Theo appears to be arrogant sometimes, or a little above everyone else, but he knows a lot, and somewhere inside of him, I believe Theo *cares* just as much as he *knows*. Anyway, he is a walking encyclopedia, and you can never have too much *knowledge*. We need him."

Marathon Bear

"*Marathon* would be at the top of anyone's list," Shadrack said. "Marathon is the best, all-around athlete, 'we-can-win' bear I've ever known. He's also learned that he could be a good athlete and also get high grades in school at the same time, so when we need an all-around-achiever, Marathon is our bear."

Scuba Bear

"From what the sciencebears learned by tracking the Negatroids to the planet Earth, we know that unlike Excellence, the planet Earth is mostly covered by water," Shadrack said. "So I chose Scuba Bear to go with us because he is the best diverbear on Excellence. He has also climbed the highest peaks in the Great Bear mountain range, and he cares a lot about nature and wildlife. And it looks like Earth could use some help saving the ecosystem on their planet. It's kind of a mess."

Whisper Bear

"Whisper may be quiet and shy," Shadrack said, "but she has an inner spirit and strength that shouts—even if you can't always hear it out loud. She will be an inspiration for everyone on the team, and she is one kidbear who will *never* give in to the negatives of a Negatroid. Whisper," Shadrack said, smiling, "is our secret weapon. She is a shy, quiet, but *very* strong bear. Wait till you see what Whisper can do," Shadrack concluded.

Eli had not at all expected to see the final name Shadrack had chosen, and when he read the list, it had caught him by surprise.

Eli Bear

"I would also, with respect, choose you, sir," Shadrack said. "You would not be the last of my choices to be a member of the team that goes to Earth. You would be my first."

"And why, among your young friends, would you choose me to go with you?" old Eli responded.

"I would choose you to be part of the team," Shadrack said, "because although the rest of us have a lot of team spirit, and we have the youthful strength and stamina it will take to fight the Negatroids, we need one bear who has age and wisdom, who can give us the guidance to succeed."

Adding Eli to the list was not a move for favor on Shadrack's part. Shadrack was a very smart bear. He knew what he needed to have with him if he was to travel to the planet

Earth, have any chance of helping the kids who lived there, defeat the Negatroids, and make it safely back home.

Old Eli understood what Shadrack was doing in bringing each member of his team together. Other than his own name being on the list, the scroll from the Great Bear had foretold it. But he immediately understood the reasoning behind Shadrack also choosing a wise, older, experienced bear like himself to go with them.

Eli, as he always did, looked prominent and presidential, strong and thoughtful, as he spoke. "As unusual as it would be for me to agree to join you, when I have so much to do here on Excellence, and as difficult as it would be to leave our beautiful planet behind for a time . . . I will go with you," Eli said.

"But you, Shadrack, will lead the mission to Earth. I will be there. I will help you in any way I can. But it will be you, and your Self-Esteem Team, who have to fulfill the mission, stop the Negatroids, and help the children of Earth."

Then, reviewing the list a final time, Eli said, "Earth could certainly use some help right now. Perhaps we can help the children of Earth discover the *'excellence' they already have within them.* It's settled, then," he said. "You have your team. I'll issue the directive that allows each of the bears of *The Self-Esteem Team* to be excused from their normal classes at school and begin preparation for your mission."

"How much time do we have to prepare?" Shadrack asked. "When do you think the Negatroids will begin their attack on planet Earth?"

"Get the Self-Esteem Team ready," Eli said. "We must prepare as rapidly as we can. We believe that even now, as we speak, the terrible Negatroids have started their attack on the children of Earth. *The battle for their spirits has already begun.*"

Chapter Nine

The Attack on Planet Earth

Eli's prediction was correct. In the darkening sky above the planet Earth, the Negatroids were already launching their first attack.

Phase I had started. Little Earth kids, so unknowing, their parents so unsuspecting, were, one by one, losing their spirits to the dark, negative, Negatroid thoughts that were entering their minds.

When the Negatroids swooped down in their first sniper-like attacks, and began to speak their words of failure into the minds of the children of Earth, no one on Earth realized what was happening to them. No one did anything to stop the terrible negative words of self-defeat and failure that their children were being hit with, because they didn't even know the invisible Negatroids were there.

How could they know? The same kinds of negative thoughts that the terrible Negatroids were now putting into the little Earth kids' minds were the same kinds of words that many of those kids had been hearing, word after word, day after day, from grownup humans, other kids, and the world all around them, for all the years of their lives.

Again and again, they heard the negative words and messages from parents who should have known better, but didn't.

They heard the negative words and thoughts from some of the teachers at school who were negative themselves, and who passed their own negativity on to the children they were supposed to be helping succeed.

They heard them from bullies on the playground, kids with low self-esteem and poor parenting, who took their anger out on the kids around them.

They saw and heard the destructive, negative messages in video games that were filled with non-stop killing and violence. And they heard the negative messages in movies and television programs that were designed to hypnotize and *control* kids' minds rather than *build* them and help them.

All of these, and more, were unknowingly feeding the kids of Earth with the worst, most negative kinds of thoughts and thinking that anyone could ever imagine. Few of the grownups were even aware they were already doing it, and now the hidden whispers of the dark, shadowy Negatroids were *helping them do it*.

Like programming little human computers, word after word, negative thought after negative thought, the Negatroids programmed the *worst possible thoughts, ideas, and beliefs*, relentlessly into the receptive minds of the children they were attacking.

Negatroids, who in their normal state were dark, shadowy, ghost-like creatures, had the ability to disguise themselves to look like anyone they wanted to imitate.

When they said their negative words, the Negatroids disguised themselves as unhappy or tired parents, thoughtless, negative, or uncaring teachers, or even kids who pretended to be their friends but weren't really *friends* at all . . . it would be *Negatroids* in disguise!

The words and thoughts the Negatroids whispered into little kids' minds were always bad. Over and over again, they repeated negative, destructive, incredibly harmful words and thoughts like:

You can't do anything good!
You're nothing!
Why would you even try?
I hate you!
I wish you had never been born!
You're so stupid!
I can never count on you!
You always make mistakes!
You'll never amount to anything!

Why can't you do anything right?
I don't believe a thing you say.
You're just like your father!
Don't bother me, I'm busy.
Who do you think you are?
You don't know how to tell the truth.
I can never count on you.
And on, and on, and on . . .

Word by word, negative thought by negative thought, *tens of thousands* of the terrible Negatroids had begun their attack, programming the Earth kids' minds with negatives. It was mental and emotional abuse of the worst kind—and it was working.

Within days of their first entry into the children of Earth's already tattered and frayed sense of "self," the Negatroids dove deeper, finding every flaw in every child they attacked, changing their night-time dreams from *good* and *wonderful* and being *secure*, to nightmares of *fear* and *being lost forever*.

Little six-year-old Kendal, for the first time in his life, dreamed that a *demon* had entered his bedroom and hovered above him, putting terrible thoughts into his mind, and terrifying him until dawn. It wasn't a demon, of course. It was a *Negatroid*, stealing the positive dreams away from little Kendal, and replacing them with *negative, evil, fear*, and *bad*.

When she talked to her mother, twelve-year-old Stephanie was about to tell the truth about why she hadn't gotten her homework done on time, when all of a sudden, a great, dark, swooping *lie* came into to her mind, and instead of just telling the truth to her mother, Stephanie found herself saying something that she knew was a lie, the opposite of the truth.

The completely unnecessary lie that came to her, was not hers at all, of course. It was a Negatroid, determined to change her words from the truth to a lie. Kids weren't born knowing how to lie. It was something they had to learn. And the Negatroids were all too happy to teach them.

When young Jason, who had always been a good kid, and never in his life been cruel or a bully, taunted Patricia, the girl in his third-grade class, and told her over and over that she was a "Fatty-Patty," a part of him knew that it was wrong to say anything like that.

But another, totally new part of Jason's mind got him to do it anyway. The Negatroid who was programming the negative "Fatty Patty" thoughts into Jason's young mind didn't care how much his words would hurt little Patricia, maybe for the rest of her life.

All the evil, shape-shifting Negatroid who was programming Jason's mind with unkindness cared about was turning Jason into someone bad instead of someone good.

"I've got him now! I've got this Earth kid named Jason. I'll stay with him and keep doing this. *With enough repetition of bad thoughts, in a few days, I'll have his mind. And in time, I'll have his spirit.* Little Jason *is going to the Nozone."*

That is the sad, but never-relenting way Negatroids *think*. And before the bears of Excellence could help the Earth kids defend themselves, that's the way thousands and thousands of Negatroids descended, and then attacked, one-on-one, the thoughts and minds of the children of Earth.

Phase I of their evil plan to destroy the children of Earth with the constant repetition of *negative* was underway! What should have been the little children's mental programs of *good,* were being rewired by the Negatroids, and becoming programs of *bad.*

Chapter Ten

Self-Talk for Self-Defense

It would be only two short days after Eli asked Shadrack to form the Self-Esteem Team, that Shadrack was called back to the Science and Technology Cave.

"I have brought you here to meet with the other bears of Excellence who have agreed to help us on our journey to Earth," old Eli said. "As I'm sure you know, the Self-Esteem Team cannot do what we want to do—save the children of planet Earth—entirely on our own." And with that, old Eli presented the additional bears who would go with them to support their mission.

"As you know, this is Sazza Bear. Sazza has bear degrees in science, biotechnology, and medicine. She is one of the greatest sciencebears, and most important bears on the planet Excellence. And she agreed to come with us because she saw what was happening on planet Earth, and she knows that keeping the Negatroids from destroying Earth will not be easy.

"Next is Kim Bear, whom you know well, since he often coaches rolley. Kim is a renowned technobear, and will be the captain of the *Starship Excellence* on its way to planet Earth. Once there, he will interface with *Earth Base I*, which we will set up on the planet's surface."

"I have also asked Mandelbright Bear to join us because he is one of the best "thinking" bears we have on the planet Excellence. He has a remarkable ability to see both the big picture, and at the same time, all of the smallest details. And, by the way, he asks that you call him 'Mandy.'

"After we arrive at our destination, Sazza, Kim, and Mandy will remain in orbit above the planet Earth, while The Self-Esteem Team members land in the Star Point Shuttles and set up *Earth Base I*. Everything we're doing on the planet's surface will be monitored by our three friends here, and we'll be counting on them to help make our mission a successful one."

After Shadrack was introduced to the *Starship Excellence* crew, and they had discussed how they would coordinate their efforts during the days ahead, Eli excused Shadrack to return to his teammates who were already well into their training in preparation for their departure for planet Earth.

There was a great deal to do, and every member of The Self-Esteem Team was working hard to get it done.

* * * * * * * * * * * *

Interest in the ancient art of *Self-Talk for Self-Defense* had come very much alive again after it had helped the bears defeat the Negatroids when they had attacked Excellence.

Now, preparing for the worst from the Negatroids when they would meet them again on planet Earth, the bears of the Self-Esteem Team practiced the positive art form for hours each day as their departure day drew closer.

Every day, many of the parentbears and kidbears of Excellence would go to the rolley field to watch Shadrack and the members of the Self-Esteem Team practice. They were working on the graceful forms, the precision steps, and the powerful words of *Self-Talk for Self-Defense.* They hoped that perfecting their skills would help the bears when they once again met the Negatroids.

One of the exercises practiced by the members of the team was called **"Negative/Positive."**

In this exercise, anytime any team member shouted out a negative word or phrase, another member had to instantly shout out the opposite—the *positive* form of the same word or phrase.

If one of them shouted out a word like "*impossible*," another team member would immediately shout back, "***very possible***." If someone shouted, "*cannot*," another bear would shout back, "***can!***" If one of them shouted, "*You're nothing!*" another team member would immediately shout, "***I am everything—everything good!***"

Now, in a remarkable team exercise, the loudspeakers in Great Bear Stadium had been turned up loud, and as the members of The Self-Esteem Team stood at the far end of the field, facing forward, the loudspeakers began to blare negative thought after negative thought toward the team of bears.

"*You are nothing! You are worthless! You are no one!*" the loudspeakers shouted at the bears, like invisible Negatroids on the attack.

"I am more than something! I have value! I am someone who counts!" the bears shouted back.

As they shouted out the words, the bears moved in perfect timing and precision steps, turning gracefully, one arm outstretched, one knee slightly bent, the other arm now crossing to the front, deflecting the words of negative. Now, still in unison, they stepped forward, turning again.

"You will fail, and you cannot win!" the loudspeakers bellowed.

"We choose to win, and we do not fail!" the Incredibears shouted back in unison.

"You cannot beat the Negatroids, and you cannot succeed!" the loudspeakers blared even louder.

"We overcome all Negatroids and we will succeed!" the bears of The Self-Esteem Team shouted as one.

Then, forming a perfectly straight line, facing toward the practice Negatroid-like loudspeakers at the far end of the field as a barrage of scurrilous negative words were hurled toward them in a non-stop torrent, the Self-Esteem Team began to run forward in a solid line.

From the loudspeakers at the other end of the field came the words *"Impossible, negative, cowardly, uncaring, pain, anguish, failure, worthless, quit, hopeless, suffering, darkness, fear, despair,* and *defeat . . ."* the negative words thundered at them.

As they ran, the Self-Esteem Team shouted out a powerful cheer of the *opposite* kinds of words. In perfect harmony, and running forward, they shouted out the Incredibear words of *winning*: **"Belief! Attitude! Spirit! Value! Courage! Bravery! Confidence! Integrity! Caring! Quality! Faith! Determination! Endurance! Achievement!** and **Success!"**

As the line of Self-Esteem Bears roared forward on the field, shouting out the powerful words of *winning*, the blaring loudspeakers themselves seemed to almost pivot and move backwards on their stands.

The bears of the Self-Esteem Team were getting ready . . . and they were getting very *good*.

      * * * * * * * * * * *

Finally, but all too quickly, it was time to leave. Eli told Shadrack to let the team members know it was time to say their goodbyes to their families and friends. They would have just one more night to make their final preparations, and on the next day they would leave.

The night before their departure, Shadrack asked the members of the Self-Esteem Team to meet him, away from the others, for just a short while. He had something he wanted to talk with them about.

It was not unusual that Shadrack wanted the team members to meet him on his favorite hillside. That was where he had spent so many thoughtful hours looking at the stars in the nighttime sky.

This night, the sky seemed to be more brilliant than ever, as the team members sat on the grassy hillside together, sitting in a circle, looking at the star-filled heavens above them.

Holly was there, and so, too, were Theo and Believer Bear. Theo was more humble than usual, the vastness of the starlit sky overshadowing his need to be intellectual at the moment. Believer Bear was almost always playing a role of some kind or other, but not now. He, too, seemed to sense the importance of the role all of them were about to play in real life.

Wheely was in his little wheel chair, and for once he was sitting quietly, and not darting and swiveling around like he usually was. Scuba Bear sat quietly, wearing his clear diving bubble as always, looking through it at the sea of stars above them.

Marathon was there, but unusual for him, he was not dribbling an invisible basketball or making invisible hoop shots. He just sat quietly on the grassy hillside, looking upwards with the others.

Poppy Bear, instead of doing cartwheels, was sitting quietly with Whisper, both of them staring into the depths of the sky above them as though they were really looking at it for the first time ever.

"Right . . . *there,*" Shadrack said, standing and pointing to an almost dark patch of sky that was home to the planet they would be traveling to. "Way up there, in that part of the galaxy, is the planet Earth," he said. "And it's because of Earth, and what's happening there, and why we're going there, that I wanted to talk to you."

Shadrack was a good team-leader. Old Eli had chosen well. But even though he was responsible for his team, Shadrack was very cautious to never be "preachy," even when he had something important to say.

"I know, by now, each of you has asked yourself the question, 'Why are we going to some planet far away to help kids we don't even know?' And I suppose each of you has come up with your own answer. I know it could be for the adventure that's in front of you, or it could be because it's exciting going into space, or it could be that you were asked to go, and you feel it's your duty . . . or it could be any reason at all. I just wanted to say thank you to all of you. We're the team, and I'm glad that each of you is part of this team."

It was the longest speech Shadrack had ever made. And even though it sounded a little like one of the pep-talks the rolley coaches often gave them, it had a deeper meaning.

All of them sat together under the massive starlit sky, with a destination that was very very far away, and no promises about what they would find when they got there, or even whether they would be successful, or if they would ever see Excellence again.

Each of them knew that this wasn't at all like a game of rolley that would end with both teams shaking hands at the end of the game, and everyone going home to dinner. This was different. This was real. And the reason for going, for each of them, was very important.

"Do you mind if I chime in?" a voice said from out of the darkness beyond the circle of team members. It was Eli, whom Shadrack had also asked to join them. When he appeared, Shadrack, out of respect for the elderbear, stepped back, and stood silently, waiting for Eli to speak.

"Along with thanking each of you for being a member of Shadrack's team, there are just two things I want to say to you. Then, I think we will all be ready to leave on our journey," Eli said.

"First, in going to Earth with the hope of helping the children of Earth, each of you has found a purpose. In doing that, you are finding something that many of us search a lifetime to find—that is: a *reason* for *being*.

"For your purpose in life, by joining this team, you have chosen to help others. *You will never find a purpose that is greater than that of being of service to others.*

"Second, and just as important, the most lasting part of your journey will not only be in what you do when you get there. It will be in what you learn, and how much you grow, within yourself. *The finding and the strengthening of your own inner spirit will be your true journey.*"

None of the bears, including Shadrack, said a word. There was nothing more that was needed. They all understood. And they were all ready.

Chapter Eleven

The *Starship Excellence*

The next morning, dawn found the *Starship Excellence,* gleaming brilliantly in the first rays of the morning sun, awaiting the Self-Esteem Team, and ready to go.

The giant golden ship that would take the Self-Esteem Team to Earth, glistened so beautifully in the morning sunlight for a very good reason—the entire surface of the large, star-shaped craft was covered in 24 karat *gold*. Unlike on many planets, gold was plentiful on Excellence, and the bears made good use of it.

Conceived by the Great Bear himself, the *Starship Excellence* had a unique and very practical design. First off, the huge ship was built in the shape of a perfect five-pointed star. In the center of the star was a large pentagon-shaped hub that held the ship's control room, galley, general area, training and workout area, and storage bays.

Attached to the central pentagon-shaped hub, each of the five "star points" was a complete self-contained and self-powered space shuttle. Each "Star Point Shuttle" could hold multiple passengers, and included sleeping berths, maintenance space, and equipment bays.

After *Starship Excellence* arrived at a stationary position above Earth, each of the star point shuttles could "undock" from the central hub, called *"Space Base I,"* and travel to anywhere on the planet.

When all of the Star Point Shuttles undocked, and left to go on a mission, *Space Base I*, then a golden pentagon with no points, would remain in orbit above the planet, monitoring the activities of each of the shuttles during its mission. When the star points returned, and reattached themselves,

Space Base I would be transformed into a beautiful, glistening golden five-pointed star once again—the *Starship Excellence.*

* * * * * * * * * * *

Now, on departure day, the bear families of Excellence gathered excitedly around the huge golden starship, where it waited for its important crew and passengers in the middle of Great Bear Stadium. The huge arena was now packed with bears. The bears of Excellence had come to see The Self-Esteem Team off on their important journey to save the children of Earth from the terrible Negatroids.

When Shadrack and The Self-Esteem Team arrived at the stadium, a roaring cheer went up from the throngs of bears and bear families gathered there to see them off.

Even the precious little Flub and Blunder, two wonderful but not yet quite balanced and coordinated little bears, rollicked and rolled, laughing and stumbling, fumbling this way and that, trying to get as close as they could to the beautiful golden starship. Flub and Blunder wanted to say goodbye to their friendbears who were boarding the ship, friends that they thought were just going to fly away and have *fun!* Little Flub and Blunder wanted to go *too!*

It was hard for some of the team members themselves to get to the entrance of the great gleaming ship—as they were being given endless, teary-eyed bearhugs by overly-worried and endlessly-proud parentbears and familybears.

In the last moments, as the team members boarded, there was a great hubbub at the boarding door, as the family bears packed in as close as they could, eyes glistening with tears, waving into the interior, and shouting out wishes and blessings and goodbyes to their loved ones on board.

But finally, Shadrack and Eli and all of the team members were inside the starship, the entrance door was closed, and the Self-Esteem Team and the crew of technobears were ready to go.

"Is everyone set for takeoff?" Captain Kim asked, his deft paws moving confidently over the controls in front of him. Then, glancing down at his clipboard, he said, "Roll call, starting with the Self-Esteem Team."

"*Wheely Bear,*" Kim said loudly.

"*On top, in tune, in touch, and going for it,*" Wheely said, shouting out one of the phrases of self-talk the bears had been rehearsing each day. And then he said, "*Present . . .* and so is my gear," he added, referring to the special turbocharged wheelchair he had made sure was on board.

"*Holly Bear,*" Kim continued.

"Yup! Here," Holly answered.

"*Believer Bear.*"

"*Captain Verne Stevens of the first Earth Mission Brigade, present and accounted for,*" Believer Bear answered, in the perfect strong voice of an imaginary character he had created in his mind.

"*Poppy Bear,*" Captain Kim said next, going down his list.

"Here with cheer!" Poppy shouted out, full of enthusiasm.

"*Theo Bear.*"

"Present in the physical location we subjectively perceive to be '*here,*'" Theo said, exactly as you would expect Theo to answer.

"*Marathon Bear,*" Kim said next.

"*On board, on the team, and ready to win!*" Marathon shouted back.

"*Scuba Bear,*" Kim continued.

"This is no *submarine*, but I'm *here*," Scuba said with a grin.

"*Whisper Bear,*" Kim said.

After a long silence, Kim said again, louder this time, "*Whisper Bear!*"

"Whisper is saying '*here,*'" Holly Bear said. "You just can't hear her."

During the roll call, Captain Kim could have called out the names of the three Positronic bears, *Polaris, Ursus,* and *Major,* but he would have gotten no response. These were the very special robotic bears that had been created by the technobears to defend the bears of Excellence from the terrible Negatroids. The three giant robotic bears were on board, but shut down, in "sleep" mode for the voyage. They would be activated after the starship reached planet Earth.

Captain Kim continued the roll call.

"*Eli Bear,*" he said, very respectfully.

"*I am here with you,*" Eli answered solemnly.

Then Kim moved on to the two bears, who, along with him, were the sciencebears on the list.

"*Sazza Bear,*" Kim said.

"*Present,*" Sazza said, "and proud of all of you."

"*Mandelbright Bear,*" Kim said, and then corrected himself. "*Mandy.*"

"*Present,*" Mandy said.

And finally, Kim said, "*Shadrack Bear.*"

"Happy to be here, and ready to go," Shadrack responded.

"Then, Shadrack, you have command of this mission," Captain Kim said, speaking directly to the leader of the Self-Esteem Team.

"Bears of the *Starship Excellence,*" Shadrack said to all of them. "*Let our journey begin.*"

* * * * * * * * * * *

Outside the great golden ship, a hush finally settled over the crowd of bears in Great Bear Stadium. They stood wide-eyed in awe as the ship suddenly began to hum softly . . . and then it began to *glow*.

Bears scrambled backward over bears as they clamored to move away from the humming, glowing starship.

They watched open-mouthed as slowly and wondrously, the ship began lifting up, humming louder and glowing brighter. Then, after hovering just above them for a few last moments, the great ship ascended until it was far above the bears in Great Bear Stadium.

Slowly, gracefully, it turned on its side, a giant, golden, five-pointed star, poised motionless in the deep, darkening blue of the late evening sky.

And then, suddenly, it swept into space, a beautiful poetic shooting star, with a long, sweeping arc of golden light trailing behind it. And then it was gone.

Shadrack and the Incredibears of the Self-Esteem Team were on their way.

* * * * * * * * * * *

Far away on planet Earth, the terrible Negatroids had no thought of Excellence, or of the bears they had tried to destroy there. Bears were *history!* Right now, the Negatroids were too busy wreaking havoc on Earth, destroying minds and wresting little kids' spirits out of them.

Phase I of their evil plan was working. Soon, with enough Negatroid sniper attacks—thousands upon thousands of them around the planet—programming the minds of little Earth kid after little Earth kid, weakening and destroying their once promising minds one by one, the Negatroids would be ready to launch *Phase II.*

Chapter Twelve

Stowaways

The technobears of Excellence had used their extensive knowledge of quantum mechanics to create a brilliantly simple drive system for the *Starship Excellence*. Its journey to Earth would not take place in a few moments, as the Negatroids' ships could do. But their drive system was still considered fast, and the Self-Esteem Team would make the entire trip in less than a week of Earth time.

During the voyage, the team members drilled relentlessly, practicing their self-talk words, steps, and forms, and giving each other endless tests and quizzes like the *"If/Then"* quizzes.

"If/Then" meant, "*If this* were to happen, *then* what would you do next? It was played as a teaching game on Excellence, but here it was being used to help each of the team members plan in advance what they would do if something unknown or unexpected happened to them while they were on planet Earth.

On Earth, each of them would most certainly have to deal with a great many unknowns. And it would help them to practice, in advance, the kind of *positive choices* they would have to make when the time came.

Holly was asking Believer Bear a question in one of the "If/Then" practice sessions.

"If a Negatroid jumped up behind you, and tried to scare you, and then shouted bad, evil, negative words into your mind, then what would you do next?" Holly asked.

"I would immediately make the Negatroid think that I was just another Negatroid, disguised as a bear," Believer said, "and I would make my face look so horrible and frightening that the Negatroid would think I was one of them, and it would go looking for someone else to attack. I would make myself look like *this*," Believer said, changing his appearance completely.

Holly smiled a bit nervously. "That's almost *too* good," she said, shocked at the sight of Believer's suddenly somewhat hideous features. "That's excellent. You'll have to remember that one," she said with a shudder.

Poppy asked Wheely the next If/Then question. "Wheely, if you were alone in the dark, and you suddenly found yourself surrounded by a *hundred* Negatroids," Poppy asked, "*then* what would you do?"

Wheely thought a moment, trying to *imagine* what being surround by a hundred Negatroids would be like.

Finally, he answered. "Well, I probably couldn't fight off all of them by myself, especially if there were a *hundred* Negatroids, so I would do the smartest thing I could do, and make tracks out of there. I'm no coward, but I think I would turn my wheelchair on 'high,' hit the turbo, and get out of there *fast*." And then Wheely added, "Let's just hope it never happens."

Scuba Bear asked Theo the next If/Then question. Scuba, as usual, was wearing a crystal clear, perfectly round diving bubble on his head during the If/Then practice sessions with the other bears. Scuba almost *always* wore his diving bubble, no matter *where* he was, or *what* he was doing.

"*If* you were very tired," Scuba asked the very intellectual thinkerbear Theo, "and nothing was going right, and everything was going wrong, and you were ready to go to sleep, and if just then the Negatroid alarm sounded and you had to jump up, and help save Earth kids from more Negatroids, what would you do?"

Theo looked at Scuba Bear oddly. "I would wonder how the cosmic universe had gotten itself so screwed up that it would have a little bear with a bubble on his head asking other bears questions like that," Theo answered. And shaking his head quizzically, he got up to leave. But just before he left, he paused. "I'd help the Earth kids," Theo said, winking at Scuba, and smiling, walked away.

Suddenly, in the midst of the team's practice session, Captain Kim walked into the group area where the crew and team held their training sessions. The Captain said to Shadrack, "We have a problem."

"What is it?" Shadrack asked, hoping nothing had gone wrong with the ship on its course to Earth.

"I'm afraid we have a couple of stowaways," Kim answered, trying to look angry, but looking more amused instead.

Suddenly both Sazza and Mandy came in, each holding a squirming, wiggling, giggling little cub bear. It was *Flub* and *Blunder!*

"How did you get here?" Shadrack asked, complete surprise showing on his face.

"*We wanted to come too!*" little Flub smiled. Or maybe it was Blunder who answered.

"Yup! *We wanted to go on a ride!*" the other little cub giggled, squirming for freedom as Mandy tried to hold him.

You really couldn't tell the two little bears apart. Their motherbear had even made special T-shirts for them to wear with "F" and "B" in big letters on the front, but the two cubs were always getting their T-shirts mixed up, so that even *she* had trouble telling them apart.

When Poppy saw the little cubs, two of her best little buddies on Excellence, she leaped up and grabbed little Blunder—or at least there was a good chance it was Blunder—and took him from Mandy. Right behind her was Wheely Bear who nabbed little Flub and did a fast 360-degree spin in his wheelchair.

The cubs were always a big hit on Excellence—*everyone* loved them. But out here in space, with the Self-Esteem Team getting ready to defend the kids of Earth from the terrible Negatroids, was definitely *not* the safest place for two little cub bears, Shadrack thought. "What we have to do on this mission is serious business."

"How did you get on board?" Shadrack asked the two little cubs.

"We're *throwaways*," Flub and Blunder shouted at once, laughing and giggling as they answered.

"They mean *stowaways*," said Believer, smiling at both of them.

"They can be our team mascots!" Holly Bear shouted out.

"I'm *glad* they're with us!" the shy, little voice of Whisper Bear chimed in, her usually small voice a little louder with the arrival of the two cubs.

While the two little cub bears bounced and frolicked, old Eli got Shadrack's attention, and motioned that he wanted to talk with him.

"What is it, sir?" Shadrack asked, ready to listen.

Old Eli bent down to tell him what he knew was important for Shadrack to hear.

"It was foretold. It's in the scrolls," he said. "The Great Bear foretold that there would be two very youngerbears, *cub* bears, who would one day help defeat the Negatroids. According to the scrolls," Eli said, "their names would be *'Fun'* and *'Wonder*,' but the story in the scrolls sounds like it was our two little stowaways.

"I have an idea," Shadrack said. "Their names today may be 'Flub' and 'Blunder,' but imagine what could happen if we accepted these two cubs as a part of our team, and made it official!"

Then, smiling his special Shadrack smile, he said, "We'll change their names! We'll change the words Flub and Blunder, which really mean doing things *wrong* and making *mistakes*, to *Fun* and *Wonder*, which mean much more positive things, like *happiness and curiosity*. The new names would be *perfect* names for little cub bear members of the Self-Esteem Team."

With a knowing look, old Eli nodded in agreement. The story in the scrolls was coming to pass.

A short time later, addressing the members of his team, Shadrack said to them, "Flub and Blunder will stay." At that announcement, all of the bears cheered happily.

"But from this day forward," Shadrack continued, "our young cub bears will no longer be known as 'Flub' and 'Blunder.' As of today, their names will be *'Fun'* and *'Wonder.'*"

"That little one, over there," Shadrack said, holding his paw toward the cub bear wearing the T-shirt with the initial *'F'* on it will now be known as *'Fun.'* And our other little friend, the one Holly is holding, who was called *'Blunder,'* will now be called *'Wonder.'*"

In giving the two cubbears new names, Shadrack had figured out an important step in making things work for kids. Give kids a positive *identity*, a *picture* of themselves that would build them *up*, and they would live up to the identity they were given.

The last thing Shadrack heard that night, before he went to sleep, was the clear young voice of Fun, saying to his friends on the *Starship Excellence*, "I used to be stupid and clumsy, but now I can be everything I wanted to be. I'm not 'Flub,' I'm *Fun*."

And his little twin cubbear brother said sleepily, "I used to always be called Blunder, and all I did was make mistakes. But now I'm *Wonder* instead. I *wonder* what I can do now," he smiled, his little bear mind already full of possibilities, as he fell fast asleep.

When Shadrack accepted the little bear cubs onto his Self-Esteem Team, little did he know that one day, in the middle of one of the greatest battles with the Negatroids, these two happy, rollicking little cubbears would be at the very center of a battle with the two most evil Negatroids ever. But that story, and much more, would come later.

Chapter Thirteen

Earth Base I

On the day of the bears' arrival, the golden *Starship Excellence* appeared in the sky just before dawn above the planned base location on planet Earth.

"We've found a secure place for the Self-Esteem Team to land and set up *Earth Base I*," Captain Kim said to Shadrack, and nodded toward the view screen that showed a clearing in the tree-covered terrain a few thousand feet below them.

The location the technobears had found for the team to make their encampment was in a place called a "National Park." The park they chose was far away from the lights and the cities of the humans of planet Earth. From their secure base location in the park, the bears would be able to travel in their individual Star Point Shuttles to anywhere on the planet, without detection. It would be a perfect place to set up *Earth Base I*.

Less than twenty minutes later, after the members of the Self-Esteem Team had made their final preparations before descending to Earth in the five Starpoint Shuttles, Shadrack nodded briefly at Eli, and then turned toward his small team of bears, and spoke.

"It's time," he said. "When the Negatroids learn we've come to Earth to stop them, they'll do everything they can to stop *us*. But we're the bears of Excellence, and we're not going to let them do that." And then he said, *"Let's go help the kids of Earth."*

* * * * * * * * * * *

Shadrack instructed his team to take their places in the shuttles. For the present, all five shuttles would be operated by remote control from *Space Base I*. For this short trip, the only thing each of the Self-Esteem members had to do was get on board the shuttle they would be manning, strap in, and sit tight for the short trip to the planet's surface below.

As soon as each of the team members was ready, the main hatches to the hub slid shut, and one by one, the Star Point Shuttles undocked from the hub and drifted free. Then, in unison, the five delta-shaped Star Points moved together and flew downward, heading silently for their destination on the surface below.

Kim, Sazza, and Mandy remained in the control center, the pentagon-shaped hub of the starship, now officially *"Space Base I,"* that would stay in space, high above the team after they landed.

* * * * * * * * * * *

The landing went without a hitch, and setting up *Earth Base I* took little time. First, each of the Star Point Shuttles had landed in a single large clearing, surrounded by towering pine trees. They landed in perfect placement, pointing outward, forming the points of a five-point star, with open space in the middle.

Next, Kim Bear, sitting in the control hub high above them, pushed a button on his control panel. As he did so, a five-paneled canopy formed over the central empty space, covering it completely, between the five, outward-pointed shuttles. When the cover canopy was in place, the grouping formed a complete "star" once again, creating an exact likeness of the *Starship Excellence*, resting on the forest floor.

Shadrack and the Self-Esteem Team were now safely hidden under a faceted dome of protection, surrounded by the five shuttles. *Earth Base I* was complete.

Now, from above them in *Space Base I*, Kim Bear began remotely activating the Positrons.

In the cargo bays of three of the landed shuttles, the giant robotic bears began to move and awaken. One by one, the Positronic robot bears moved out of the confines of the shuttles, and slowly stood to their full height, at full attention.

They were awesome bears, standing three times taller than any bear of Excellence. They immediately began to turn their great robotic bear heads, searching for anything wrong—anything *negative*.

The arms and legs of each of the Positrons were armored with deflection shields against any negative attack, and they had been pre-programmed back home on Excellence to defend the Self-Esteem Team against any Negatroid word or thought.

Captain Kim then turned the control of the Positrons over to Shadrack, who watched as the giant robotic bears went through their anti-Negatroid routines, moving, turning, deflecting Negatroid advances, and ready to defend at a moment's notice. When they were needed, the giant Positrons would be ready.

Chapter Fourteen

The *Aura Suit of Light*

Having landed safely in their shuttles, set up camp, and taken the Positrons out of hibernation, the bears of Excellence were ready, and anxious to get started.

"Let's do it! Let's find the Negatroids, shut them down, and we'll be done, and we can all go home," they told each other exuberantly. Clearly, the Self-Esteem Team members felt they were ready, even if they had no real idea what might actually lie in store for them.

"Before we go looking for Negatroids," Shadrack said, "let's do one more check of our gear."

The special equipment they would be using was laid out in front of them. "Make sure you have your wristbands, arm guards with their control panel of buttons, and leg guards," Shadrack said. "All of them are designed to deflect anything negative. These are similar to the *Negatroid Word Deflector Shields* we used on Excellence. But these are better, and have a broader deflection range.

"You all know the control panel of your armbands," Shadrack continued. "In a minute I'll explain the new control button that has been added."

"Your Incrediphones," Shadrack said, holding up the gold-colored earphones, "should stop anything from the Negatroids that gets past your deflection shields.

"Each of your backpacks contains a set of Negaviewers, like these," he said, holding up the Virtual Reality-like optical screens the bears would wear in front of their eyes. "When you put them on and flip on the infrared control, you will be able to see any Negatroid that's near you.

Then he added, "This is especially important. Use the Negaviewers only when you have to, because when they're turned on, the Negatroid can detect the beam you're sending out, and that will tell them you're there.

"Each of you also has a Negahorn, and the technobears have beefed up the power on these. Remember to only send messages that are positive when you're confronted by a Negatroid," Shadrack reminded them. "Negatroids feed on darkness, and negatives makes them stronger. But as we learned on Excellence, anything that's *positive* stops them. At least, we *hope* it stops them," he added, knowing that his team had probably not seen everything the evil Negatroids could do.

Each of the bears had also been given a small, pocket phone that would allow them to contact *Earth Base I* and *Space Base I* when they were on a search assignment in their shuttles. The phones weren't set up to work on Earth's cellphone frequencies, but each of the bears could communicate directly with their own bases.

Now, feeling totally equipped and ready for anything, the team members were impatient to get started.

But Shadrack wasn't quite ready for them to depart. "There's one more thing the technobears have developed for us," he said with a smile that showed his enthusiasm about what he was going to show them next. "And this is a very big thing," he said. "It could be a game-changer. It's an anti-Negatroid tool that none of us has seen before.

"Kim Bear," Shadrack said, speaking into his phone to Kim who sat at the control panel in *Space Base I*. "Activate the tuning generator for the *Aura Suit of Light*."

A moment later, as the members of the Self-Esteem Team watched, a small, shimmering sphere of light appeared in the center of the circle of bears. Then, as Kim turned the energy field higher, the glistening sphere of light grew in size. All of the bears stepped back as the sphere of light continued to grow even larger, and in only moments, the light grew to become a large, buzzing, humming, swirling mass of dazzling brilliant light, filled with every color imaginable.

The sphere of light now hovered, swirling and humming, taking up most of the space in the center of *Earth Base I*. And then, as they watched it swirl and glow, each of the bears began to notice something. Each one of them began to feel the most positive energy they had ever felt.

"The technobears," Shadrack said, "have captured the *spirit* of Excellence. By discovering how to tune in to the positive spirit in each of us, they have created a device that will give every team member a virtual *suit of light*. Once you've been properly tuned, or 'activated,' your natural, invisible aura of energy, the light of your own spirit that always surrounds you, will become *visible*, creating a *suit of light* that everyone will be able to see—especially the Negatroids!"

Shadrack paused to make sure all the team members understood. "The suit of light uses the energy of your own *'self'* in its most positive form. It will literally surround you with the light of your own positive thoughts. That means that when you're *'tuned in,'* and think the right, positive thoughts, each of you will become a being of *light*, the exact *opposite* of a Negatroid.

When they heard this, all of the team members suddenly became very excited, and they were eager to see the new suit of light work. "Watch this," Shadrack said. And then, without hesitating, he stepped directly into the swirling sphere of positive light, and disappeared.

The members of the Self-Esteem Team waited for Shadrack to step back out of the light. First, a few moments went by, and nothing happened. Then, it was a half a minute or more, and still the sphere of light swirled and gleamed. But Shadrack was nowhere to be seen.

And then, suddenly, Shadrack reappeared, stepping out of the light, and stood in front of them. To all the team members, he looked the same. He looked normal. "See? It's just me," he said, "but now watch this."

"Turn off all of the lights of *Earth Base I*," Shadrack communicated up to Kim Bear. A moment later, all of the lights went dark—even the bright sphere of light blinked out—and the bears stood in pitch black darkness.

"When I stepped into the energy field of the activator light," Shadrack said from the darkness, "my own *suit of light* was activated." Then, still standing in the middle of the pitch darkness, he continued, "Watch what happens when I press the gold button on my arm band, and then think just one *positive* thought. I'll think just one word. I'm going to think the word '*Excellence*.'"

And when Shadrack said the word "*Excellence*," he immediately began to glow. Standing in the darkness, Shadrack now glowed, softly lighting the area around him, and his body, itself, was the source of the light.

"Now I'm going to think a few more positive thoughts together," Shadrack said. "I'm going to think thoughts about *good* and *happiness* and *wonderful.*"

As Shadrack thought the new positive thoughts, he went from 'glowing' to 'shining' in a bright and brilliant way. Shadrack's own *thoughts* were lighting him up! They were *illuminating* him with a bright, beautiful aura of light.

"And now I'll think a lot of positive, all at the same time. I'm thinking the words *great, belief, confidence, happy, good, positive attitude, achievement and success!*" And with those words, he shined and sparkled even brighter.

And then he said the most powerful words of all . . . *"I believe in myself!"*

When Shadrack said those words, his whole being shimmered with an incredible, dazzling light. As he said the words, he became so bright and dazzling that the bears around him had to hide their eyes from the incredible light that was shining and sparkling out from him.

"When you activate your *Aura Suit of Light*," Shadrack said, "and when your own thinking is positive, you will be able to shine with the light of your own spirit. The stronger you think the thoughts, *the brighter your light will shine.*

"Remember," he added, "Negatroids love darkness, and they hate *light*. Especially the light of *goodness*. With what may be going on here on planet Earth right now, with all the darkness the Negatroids are creating, each one of you may have to be the *light*."

Shadrack then told Kim Bear, high above them in *Space Base I,* to generate the tuning activator once again, and when the large, gleaming, swirling sphere of light reappeared in the center of *Earth Base I*, Shadrack said to his team members, "It's time for you to get your own suits of light activated. Who will go first?"

Wheely was the first to immediately move forward, and he steered his wheelchair into the shimmering light. Then, one by one, Holly, Believer, Marathon, Scuba, Whisper, Theo, and Poppy, and even old Eli, one after another, took their turn stepping into the great swirling light of positive energy. And after a time, one by one, each of them stepped out again, feeling 'different,' and even more positive than ever.

After each of the bears had gone through the activator, they wanted to try out the capabilities of their new light suits for themselves. Holly Bear pressed the gold button on her arm band and then said, "I'm thinking the word *positive!*" As soon as she said the word, her entire bear being began to glow.

"I can become anything good I want to be," Believer Bear said, and went from his normal self to an incredibly bright glowing light of dozens of positive characters that flowed through his imaginative mind.

"I can be heard, and people will listen to me," little Whisper Bear said, very softly, as she usually did. And suddenly Whisper was blazing with light, standing tall and strong, and every word she spoke was loud and clear.

Echoing Shadrack's words of positive self-talk, Wheely said *"I believe in myself more than ever!"* and immediately his little bear body, and even his little wheelchair, began to shimmer and glow.

After all of the other Self-Esteem Team members had activated their *Aura Suits of Light*, and had begun practicing using them, the final two bears to step through, or more accurately, "tumble" their way through the sphere of light, were the little cub bears, Fun and Wonder.

Fun somersaulted through first, and Wonder dove in just after him. When they came out of the swirling sphere of positive light, they would be more fun and wonderful than ever.

In the days to come, when the team members were on a mission, helping kids somewhere on planet Earth, all they would have to do to activate their suits of light would be to push the special gold button on the control panel on their arm guards, and their suit of light would begin to light up the moment they started thinking positive thoughts.

"The Negatroids have had generations of time to practice using *negative* thoughts to bring darkness to kids on planets everywhere," Shadrack said to his team of Incredibears. "Now let's see how the Negatroids deal with kids like *us,* who are ready to turn on the *light!*"

Chapter Fifteen

Victoryland

After getting their Negatroid-stopping gear and activating their special suits of light, the Self-Esteem Team was ready to do everything they could do to help the kids of Earth. And they were ready none too soon.

Earth kids were being attacked every day by the devastating Negatroids. Home after home, family after family, school after school were being hit by the invisible, sniper-like, negative force of *Phase I* of the evil Negatroids' attack.

With thousands of shadowy, ghost-like Negatroids swooping down like storm clouds from the sky into every city and town, whispering their negative thoughts and dark words of badness into the minds of Earth kids, even good kids soon wavered, and then turned to bad.

Even the happiest kids stumbled, and found themselves not being happy anymore, thinking dark thoughts and saying hurtful, dark things they would never have thought or said before.

Kids who were already in trouble were even easier targets. They lost what little self-esteem they had, and eagerly joined gangs of street kids who were intent on nothing more than hurting others, and destroying anything good they could find.

Other kids who would never have thought of it before, were running away from home, sneaking off into the frightening night, not even sure where they were going, or why they were going there.

The most positive homes and families were discovering that their once safe, secure homes were no longer safe and secure. The

Negatroids' evil attack on the children was affecting them, too.

The lives of the kids of Earth were turning into turmoil, and their parents were struggling to even recognize their own children. Instead of joy, there was anger. Instead of happiness, there was fighting and misery. Instead of hope, there was belief in the worst.

It was all happening because the terrible, invisible Negatroids were *winning*. They were taking the children's positive spirits away from them, taking away the *good* and filling their minds with *bad*.

One by one, as the Negatroids drilled their negative thoughts into the minds of the little Earth kids they targeted, the children of Earth were, one by one, giving in and giving up. And one by one, their spirits were being captured and taken up into the terrible space in the dark sky above the Earth called the *Nozone*.

High above Earth, where once there had only been light and space, there was now an unhappy, gray, deepening shadow of darkness. It was the *Nozone*, the frightening, almost unimaginable place where the terrible Negatroids hid the stolen spirits of the little kids of Earth, and kept them there, huddling and shivering in the cold, eternal darkness.

* * * * * * * * * * *

"We know the Negatroids are here," Shadrack said to the team. "Our first task is to find out *where* they are. So I have assigned a target destination for each of you to check out. This first mission will be a reconnaissance mission only. If you find any Negatroids, don't let them know you're there. Just stay low, report in as soon as possible, and get back to *Earth Base I*."

After each of the team members had received their individual search assignments, they departed in the Star Point shuttles, each of them heading in a different direction, searching for the Negatroids on planet Earth. Each of the team members would search quietly, looking for any sign of Negatroids, but making sure they drew no attention to themselves.

Among the target destinations, school, playgrounds, camp grounds, and even homes would be surveilled. But for now, the Self-Esteem Team would let no one on Earth, especially the Negatroids, know they were there.

* * * * * * * * * * *

Taking off from *Earth Base I* in his star point shuttle, Wheely Bear was studying his assigned target destination. It was a giant amusement park called Victoryland, where Earth kids could go on rides and have a lot of fun.

"I don't think that's a place Negatroids would hang out," he said to himself. "It sounds like the kind of place they would want to avoid. Negatroids hate bright lights and happy kids. But I'll check it out, anyway." He would soon find out just how wrong he could be.

Only a short time later, Wheely was carefully guiding his star point shuttle silently into a dense area of trees just inside of the park's outer perimeter.

Not long after he had carefully landed the shuttle, where he was sure it would not be seen, he found himself on one of many walkways filled with hundreds of Earth kids and their parents making their way from one thrilling ride to another.

Wheely stopped to look around and get a good look at the place he had been assigned to reconnoiter. The huge amusement park was one of planet Earth's happiest, most positive places. It was filled to overflowing with thousands of little Earth kids, all having a great time having fun. They screamed in delight as they rode the many wonderful rides, and were filled with a sense of awe and wonder as they laughed and played in a world of fantasy come to life.

Wheely suspected that Shadrack had assigned him to check out the wildly busy amusement park just to make absolutely sure there were no Negatroids there, and he was pretty sure there wouldn't be any. With all the happiness, it was probably the safest place on Earth to be.

Now, after arriving at his destination, and seeing all the Earth kids having a wonderful time, he was even more certain that there was nothing to worry about. The Negatroids may be on planet Earth, but they certainly weren't anywhere near the brightly lighted park. The only thing here were parents and kids. Happy kids!

Wheely decided that since he was already here, and things looked safe and normal, he might just try out one or two of the rides for himself. He would stay vigilant, of course, and keep an eye out for anything suspicious, but it certainly wouldn't hurt to ride a few of the rides, and have some fun at the same time.

In spite of the fact that Wheely spent all of his days in a wheelchair, and couldn't walk or run, or even stand like other bears, he was an amazingly positive and energetic bear. And the fact that he couldn't walk or run like other bears had never stopped him from doing most of the things that other bears could do.

One of the many things Wheely could do well was have *fun*. And feeling lucky that Shadrack had chosen to send him here, in no time he was doing just that—having fun. He went on one ride, and then another.

Wheely loved riding great rides that looped into the sky and then came rocketing back toward the ground, twisting and twirling, and making kids shriek with delight. He was having a *great* day!

To his relief, he was happy to note that throughout the entire day, he hadn't seen a single Negatroid. Every so often he had taken out his special pair of Negaviewers from his backpack and looked around, but sure enough, *no Negatroids here.* The more fun he had been having, the less he had worried about anything bad happening.

But finally, Wheely decided he had better get back. He would take just one more ride, and then he would head back and report that there were no Negatroids in one of Earth's happiest places.

Wheely had found that he'd had no problem meeting and even fitting in with Earth kids. They thought he was one of the animal characters who were part of the attractions of the park. And as one of the park's characters, he also found that he was never asked for a ticket to ride on any of the rides! He was always ushered on to the ride with a courteous bow by one of the ride's attendants.

It was just after he had made friends with an Earth kid named Benny, who was also in a wheelchair, that Wheely first felt a small twinge of concern. The two of them were comparing wheelchairs, and how fast each of theirs could go, when Wheely suddenly stopped talking to his new friend, and began to look around. Something in the air felt wrong.

When he looked around him, he couldn't put a paw on anything being out of the ordinary, but when he looked up at the sky, he noticed that something about it looked strange for some reason.

It was normal for evening skies to lose their color and darken slowly, but, as Wheely noticed, *this* sky was darkening in an unusual way. And the more closely he looked, the more he realized that something was definitely wrong.

Still watching the strange change in the sky, noticing that it was darkening much too quickly, Wheely thought of the last words Shadrack had said to him as the members of the Self-Esteem Team had been sent out to search for the Negatroids.

"Have fun. Maybe even ride some rides. But be careful, best friend," Shadrack had said to Wheely. "I'm pretty sure Negatroids wouldn't attack an amusement park. Too many lights.

Too many kids having fun. Too much positive." But then, Shadrack had paused and said, "But it's Negatroids we're dealing with, and we don't know what they're capable of doing. Be careful!"

Now, as Wheely looked around more carefully, with Shadrack's cautionary words ringing in his head, he could tell there *was* something wrong about the rapidly waning twilight, and the suddenness of the emerging darkness.

"*Darkness*!" Wheely thought. It was a word that was almost synonymous with the word "*Negatroid.*" All these kids having a good time. Thousands of them. All of these lights. All of the great rides shooting kids up and around, shouting and screaming in delight as they rode them. Nothing should be wrong here.

But with the strange darkness suddenly descending faster and faster over Victoryland, Wheely knew something *was* wrong. And it was about to get a whole lot worse.

Suddenly, Wheely began to watch *everything*. Kids in groups, laughing, walking and running along the midway, having fun. He had never seen so many kids, or even bears, in one place at one time.

The action rides were filled with kids, yelling and screaming. The concession stands were filled with kids getting ice cream and corn dogs and other things Earth kids loved to eat. Kids everywhere, all happy, all having fun.

But then, just after the sky had turned to an unusual sooty kind of darkness, while Wheely watched anxiously, trying to look everywhere at once, something very strange and frightening began to happen.

One by one, the lights of Victoryland began to go out.

Chapter Sixteen

The Negatroids in Victoryland

As the dark, evil surge of ghost-like Negatroids descended over Victoryland, their twisting, negative forms shut out all the light in their path.

First, a few lights around the concession stands that sold ice cream and corn dogs began to blink out. Then the great midway lights, where thousands of Earth kids ran and played, shut down.

Next, as the Negatroids reached the giant spinning sky rides, each of the rides, one by one, began to slow, and then screech to a grinding stop, leaving Earth kids stranded on the top of high sloping rails of cars that moments before had been rocketing forward at high speed. Suddenly, without warning, they had slowed, and then stopped, and now hung motionless in the eerie darkness, the kids suspended in midair and hanging on for their lives.

In the space of no more than a few, totally unexpected moments, the great, exciting world of Victoryland went from total light and speed and fun, to a dwindling few lights, and then to silence . . . and then to complete and utter *darkness*.

At first, the kids who were riding the rides shouted out in protest, with some of the parents who were with them joining in. But, when darkness settled over all of them, they suddenly felt a strange sense of danger, a presence of evil that pervaded everything. What had been, only minutes before, a bright happy land of make-believe and rollicking fun, was suddenly an unknown world of uncertainty and danger.

What Wheely heard first were the cries of the littlest kids, scared, suddenly in darkness.

The next thing he heard were dozens of parents, telling their kids not to worry—"Everything will be okay," they said to their kids, trying to pretend they were safe.

Even as the parents tried to calm their children, telling them not to worry, the parents felt it too. In many visits to Victoryland, they had never seen or felt anything like what was happening now. Now, in the unnatural, coarse, soot-like darkness, they suddenly sensed that they *should* worry. And they definitely were *not* safe.

For the first time ever, Victoryland was filled with the sound of frightened children, filled with darkness, and filled with fear.

The Negatroids had arrived.

* * * * * * * * * * *

High above Victoryland, in the dark, shadow-like spaceship *Neanderthal I*, the evil Low gloated, doing his best to rub his claw-fingered hands together in glee and anticipation.

"We have successfully carried out *Phase I* of our attack on the children of Earth," he chortled, in a coughing kind of way. "We have sniper-targeted hundreds of thousands of Earth kids with our relentless words and thoughts of failure and disbelief, driving negative thoughts into their young minds, and it has worked.

"For years, Earth's parents have been so consumed with worry about their livelihoods and their silly diets and their bank accounts that they have forgotten their greatest asset, their *kids!*" Low wheezed.

"They never figured out that if they had taught their own children how to live in a *helping others* kind of way instead of a *self-centered* way," Low continued, almost choking on the words *'helping others,'* "they would have defeated us before we arrived. As it is, we are *winning*. We will take the spirits and the futures of their children from them, collect them, spirit by spirit, freeze them in the

Nozone, and own the children of Earth's shivering little souls forever."

"Our plan is working well," the evil brother No agreed, coughing the words as he spoke them. "Now, with *Phase II,* we will defeat an entire mass of kids in one flawless moment of victory—*thousands* of them in one attack, the attack that is now underway in what was, until just minutes ago, the ridiculously happy place called Victoryland.

"Once we have taken *thousands* and *thousands* of little Earth kids' spirits, *all at the same time,*" the evil No continued, "we will then take *all* of them, everywhere on planet Earth! The fear and chaos we create in Victoryland will echo throughout their world. *Everyone will be afraid!* How ironic," he added, "Victoryland will be a *victory* . . . for the Negatroids!

"And then," No finished, his ragged voice becoming even more sinister and diabolical as he spoke, "with fear and panic running rampant throughout their world, we will launch *Phase III, The Giant Voice of Doom.*

134

That will be the attack that will destroy the rest of the children of planet Earth *forever!*"

"I cannot *wait* to celebrate our success," No's equally-evil brother Low breathed harshly. "Let's see how our victorious Negatroids are doing down below. Let us see if everyone is having a wonderful time in Victoryland," he sneered, pointing one gnarled claw at a button on the control panel in the evil ship *Neanterthal I*.

* * * * * * * * * * *

As the lights of Victoryland went out, Wheely's fear that something was definitely very wrong was confirmed. He was also certain that he knew exactly what it was.

He immediately reached into his Incredibear Backpack and pulled on the special pair of Negvaviewers that allowed him to see Negatroids when their presence was close enough. The thousands of Earth kids around him in Victoryland would not see the usually invisible Negatroids, but with the Negaviewer, he would be able to spot them if there were any of them nearby.

Now, when he placed the Negaviewer over his eyes, Wheely shook his head twice to get his vision right—to make sure of what he saw. Wheely had seen the skies over Victoryland darken, and he had had that very bad *feeling*.

But now, when Wheely looked through the special lenses, he was completely unprepared for what he saw.

He had thought that he might actually see a Negatroid or two. He was actually kind of *hoping* he would. But he never expected to see *anything* like this. There weren't just one or two Negatroids. Now, in the darkness of Victoryland, he saw Negatroids everyplace he looked!

The Negatroids were everywhere!

What Wheely saw now were the most fearsome creatures he had ever seen. And the dark, evil, ghost-like creatures were literally everyplace he looked—*thousands of them!* Swooping and darting, swirling and swooshing, they surrounded all of the children of Victoryland, weaving in and around them, their shrill whispered words of evil sounding like a cold harsh wind, an endless keening scream of loss and despair.

The Negatroids *oozed* negative. It spun out from them like a thousand swirling fingers of darkness, luring every positive child into its grasping claws of fear and helplessness.

The silence that was created by the huge fast rides of the amusement park coming to a standstill was suddenly filled with a sound that would frighten the heart of any mother or father of any kid on Earth. It was the whimpering, pleading sound of children in peril. It was the harsh wind of danger, and the sound of *fear*, come to life.

The ruthless, evil Negatroids had brought with them the thoughts, words, and terrifying images that each child's worst fears were made of. The shadowy, ghost-like, unkind and uncaring Negatroids swept over and through the frightened masses of the children in Victoryland like nightmares that had come to life. It was as though every demon from every closet, every creature from under every bed, had been unleashed in Victoryland all at once.

No *wonder* the children were frightened. It wasn't just the sudden darkness that had closed in around them; it was the frightening terror of the words and thoughts and pictures that were being driven into their minds. Suddenly, without warning, for the thousands of children who were there, *Victoryland* was becoming *failureland*.

Chapter Seventeen

Wheely

The moment he saw what he saw, without having to think twice, in the middle of the total, oppressing blackness of Victoryland, Wheely raised his left arm in front of him. On his armband were the special buttons that glowed brightly—at the moment, the *only* light in Victoryland.

Wheely pushed a first button, and then, without pausing, he pushed a second button, the one that glowed bright gold. The moment he pushed the second button, in the middle of the total dark of Victoryland, Wheely began to "glow." He had just activated his *Aura Suit of Light*.

Since Wheely knew that the strength of the glow, the brightness of his aura, depended on the *thoughts* he was *thinking*, he immediately began to think the most positive thoughts he could imagine.

"Good," *"like,"* *"help,"* *"belief,"* and *"win,"* were some of the words he had learned that automatically came to Wheely's mind. As he thought the words, all of them positive, the light he gave off immediately grew *brighter*.

As Wheely began to glow more brightly, he saw something that surprised him. The glow from his lightsuit was beginning to light up the entire area around him. And what that light showed were the Negatroids who were moving in toward him and beginning to circle him and his little wheelchair.

Wheely snatched his Negaviewer off his head—and the Negatroids were still there! The glow from his lightsuit had made the Negatroids become *visible*. Even without the Negaviewer, you could *see* them!

Turning rapidly to look to each side, and quickly swiveling around to look behind him, Wheely saw the hateful, vicious Negatroids swarming forward, *toward* him, from everywhere! They *saw* him, they *knew* he was there, and they were coming for him!

As he saw their hideous, ghost-like faces with their evil yellow-green slits of eyes, all coming toward him in a swirling weaving motion, he could hear their coarse, wheezing, whispering voices, and he was hit from all sides by the most negative force of destructive words and thoughts that had ever been anywhere close to his mind.

The onslaught of negatives, now coming from so many Negatroids, all at once, was even stronger than the volume of stinging, hurting words that had been hurled at the bears by the Negatroids back on Excellence.

Immediately slapping his Incrediphones over his ears, protecting himself as well as he could from the words that rushed in and swirled around him, Wheely thought, "What if there are too many of them? What if I can't stop them?"

The moment he thought the words of *doubt*, the glow from his suit of light began to flicker and dim. "What if I can't do this?" he thought. And then, when he thought the words, *"What if I'm not strong enough!"* his light went out completely.

Even with his Incrediphones and his special armor that deflected many of them, the onslaught of negative words and images was so great that they screeched and screamed their way into Wheely's young mind.

Sitting alone in a wheelchair in the middle of Victoryland, surrounded by thousands of scared, frightened children, and now also surrounded by the swirling mass of attacking Negatroids, Wheely's first thought, when his lightsuit went dark, immediately took him back to the "If/Then" exercise game he had played with Poppy just a few days ago.

Poppy had asked Wheely, *"If you were alone in the dark, and you suddenly found yourself surrounded by a hundred Negatroids, then what would you do?"*

Wheely remembered his answer. He had told Poppy that since he probably couldn't fight off all of the Negatroids by himself, the smartest thing he could do would be to get out of there, fast.

"Would that be the right answer now?" Wheely thought, hurriedly. Things were different in the real world—not at all like they were in the game. And there weren't just a hundred Negatroids surrounding him. Now, in the real world, there were *thousands* of Negatroids swirling around him.

"Would I leave, and get out of here fast?" Wheely thought. But he didn't have to think about it twice.

"Not on your life!" Wheely shouted out loud. Loud enough that every Negatroid near him could hear.

Then, grabbing his Negahorn and turning the volume all the way on *high*, Wheely shouted out, *"Good, positive, strong, joyful, winning!"* loud enough for everyone to hear. *"Great belief, super goal, awesome attitude, non-stop determination, and absolute incredible confidence!"*

Without pausing, Wheely repeated the words again, as loud as he could shout them out. *"Great belief, super goal, awesome attitude, non-stop determination, and absolute incredible confidence!"*

And then he added, shouting out, *"Exceptional, positivity, amazingly good, quality spirit, kindness, purpose, value, heartfelt joy, unlimited positive possibilities,"* and *"I'm on top, in tune, in touch and going for it!"*

The words Wheely shouted, that may have been bewildering to the children of Victoryland, were the powerful words of positive self-talk that the Self-Esteem Team had been practicing so diligently every day. When Wheely shouted them out, two amazing things happened.

First, his lightsuit immediately went from dark to light again, and then to bright . . . and then to *dazzling!* Wheely looked like the *sun* had suddenly entered Victoryland.

In the same moment, the rush of attacking Negatroids surrounding Wheely immediately began to hesitate, then draw back, and then falter, stopping, back-peddling, stumbling in the air, running backwards into each other in an attempt to retreat and flee.

The positive words and thoughts Wheely had shouted out, amplified by the Negahorn, was literally pulling the evil energy out of the Negatroids and turning it into nothing but air that fell to the ground like a black, sooty kind of dust.

And along with the positive words, there was the *light*. The almost magical light that Wheely's light suit was now giving off was not *ordinary* light. It was light that was created by the overwhelming spirit of *good*—it was the powerful energy of positive *thoughts* from Wheely himself.

When Wheely thought his most positive, and shone his brightest, his light was so brilliant you almost couldn't make out the little bear himself, in his little wheelchair in the center of the beaming dazzling light, full of every brilliant color in the rainbow.

The light that was Wheely was so bright that it lit up the entire area of Victoryland around him. The children, speechless and transfixed by what was playing out in front of them, now saw the almost shapeless, ghost-like forms of the Negatroids as they swirled and twisted, keeping a safe distance from the dazzling light in the wheelchair in the center of them.

The kids of Earth were able to see, for the first time, the evil Negatroids that had been attacking them. And they were also able to see the brightly beaming little bear that was holding them off.

They watched, mesmerized, as a few of the most evil Negatroids, trying to shield their hideous yellow-green eyes from the light of good, forced themselves with the strength of pure evil, to move back in closer to Wheely, just as bullies do, taunting him, refusing to give up.

"Is that all you can do?" they screeched, "Say *words* and get *bright*? Is that *it*?"

"No," Wheely said, "there is something *else* I can do."

"And what is that?" the Negatroids wheezed back at him, still taunting, more of them getting braver, moving in, closer to the wheelchair where little Wheely sat.

"You're nothing but a toy," one of the more daring Negatroids screeched at the little bear in the wheelchair in front of him. "You talk like a giant of strength, but you have no strength at all. You can create light around your small, unimportant crippled little self, but that is all you can do!"

"No, that's *not* all I can do," Wheely said to the Negatroid bully who was taunting him. And then he paused, ready to do what he did best.

"*I can do this!*" he said.

And suddenly, the brilliantly gleaming, sparkling light that was Wheely, was no longer sitting at rest in the middle of Victoryland.

In an *instant,* the light shot forward, right into the center of the swirling mass of Negatroids, sending them screeching and scattering in all directions.

And then, just at fast, the wheelchair of dazzling, twirling light shot in another direction, and then another, cavorting and turning, spinning and wheeling at high speed, this way and that, until all the Negatroids around him were a shrieking, fleeing mass of total confusion and disarray. *Little Wheely was very good in a wheelchair.*

Darting and turning, speeding and careening, the light in the wheelchair dove in and out, showering the confused mass of Negatroids with brilliant rays and shimmering sparkles of light, blinding them with the light of good, and causing the Negatroids to scatter for safety in every possible direction.

* * * * * * * * * * *

Far above Earth, in the Negatroid command ship *Neanterthal I*, the evil Low and his brother No looked down on the scene below them in shock and dismay.

"Who is this?" the evil No screeched. "*What is this?*" he croaked, almost choking on his own words. "The destruction of the children of Earth was supposed to go *perfectly!*

"Who is powerful enough to foil our plans for the destruction of the children of Earth?"

"It's hard to see," said his evil brother Low, "so much *bright*, so much *light*. Too much light. *I hate light*," he coughed, "but it looks, as unthinkable as it would be to imagine, that there is a *bear* shouting *positives* and destroying our Negatroids on the ground. It's a *bear* in a *wheelchair!*"

"You're *insane!*" No screamed back at his brother Low. "We're on *Earth!*" he screeched. "The only bears on Earth are either wild or they're in cages in zoos! It *can't* be a bear. Not in Victoryland! It must be someone *pretending* to be a bear. Send the command to annihilate him . . . *it*, whatever it is," he wheezed.

"*Destroy the bear, or whatever it is, in the wheelchair,*" the command came down to the Negatroids on Earth.

But at that moment, with most of the Negatroids on the ground retreating, or swirling, confused, just above it, instead of following the command, the only thing they could do was try to regain their bearings.

The great glistening light in the turbocharged wheelchair moved too fast, and its showering light of positive words and thoughts disrupted every negative thought and plan of attack the Negatroids had prepared. For several glorious, shimmering minutes, the light that was Wheely spun, and stormed, and scattered the Negatroids like a cyclone.

* * * * * * * * * * *

Then, just as suddenly as it had started, the dazzling bright light sat once again in the middle of Victoryland, quietly giving off beautiful colored sparks and little beams of light.

Nearly exhausted from their frightened flurry of being chased by some shining bear-like being in a wheelchair, one of the Negatroids, wheezing heavily, trying to catch his ragged breath, finally said to Wheely. "So, maybe we won't steal your soul this time. We'll have to do that another day. But even though you may have saved yourself for now, there are plenty of other spirits here to steal."

The Negatroid who spoke moved a shadowy arm in a sweeping gesture toward the children of Victoryland around them, and said to Wheely, "You may be able to protect yourself with words and light, but the rest of the children remain in darkness, helpless and ready to be taken by us. And there is *nothing* you can do to stop us," the Negatroid wheezed, still trying to catch his ragged breath, his eyes glowing evilly.

"Well, actually, there is *one more thing* I can do," Wheely said.

"And what is that?" the Negatroid asked, ready to end the conversation and get back to the attack on the children around them.

In response, Wheely raised his left armband in front of him, and nodded toward a button that was blinking brightly. "I can do *this*," he said," and pushed the button. "*I can invite my friends.*"

Chapter Eighteen

The Incredibears in Victoryland

It was only seconds after Wheely had pressed the blinking button on his armband, that Shadrack appeared.

Earlier, when Wheely had pushed the first glowing button on his armband, Shadrack had been alerted, and he had arrived in time to see the amazing show of light, speed, and courage Wheely had used to single-handedly turn the Negatroids' attack back on themselves.

When he first arrived, Shadrack hadn't immediately turned on his own suit of light. But when he turned it on now, the Negatroids suddenly saw not just one, but *two* light beings in their midst. And the second light being was even brighter that the first! When Shadrack turned on his light suit, the space around him glowed and shined with an intensity of light that none of the Negatroids had ever seen. Shadrack's light was *blinding*.

Cowering back, trying to hide their evil yellow-green eyes from Shadrack's light, the Negatroids receded a little. They wanted to fight, but this new "light being" that stood in front of them now was something totally unexpected.

"Could it be an 'angel?'" they asked themselves. The kind of 'angel' their evil leaders had told them could not possibly exist?

After Shadrack appeared, shining brightly, beside Wheely, who was still shining super brightly on his own, the Negatroids who had been maintaining most of their negative force around the children of Victoryland began to leave their posts.

For the moment, they stopped injecting bad things into the minds of the kids, and began to swarm toward the two, bright, shining bears, Wheely and Shadrack.

"Forget the Earth kids, *kill the light*," the evil ghost-like forms of the Negatroids screamed as they swooped and coiled themselves toward the center of Victoryland, and the battle between good and evil that was taking place there.

In the midst of it all, one amazing, brilliant countenance of light, Shadrack, turned to the other dazzling, sparkling center of light, Wheely, and asked, "How are you doing, my best friend?"

"*Bear trust forever*," the sparkling light of Wheely said.

"Would you like to get rid of these Negatroids, and set these Earth kids free?" Shadrack asked Wheely.

"Ready when you are," Wheely answered. And then he repeated the powerful, positive words of self-talk they had all learned so well, "*I'm on top, in tune, in touch, and going for it!*"

"Okay, then," Shadrack said, knowing that thousands of angry warlike Negatroids were swirling around them.

As he said this, the seething wrath of the Negatroids grew, prepared to do anything they could do, and use every evil they knew, to defeat the two shining images that were trying to stop them from stealing the minds and the spirits of the children of Earth.

As the Negatroids regrouped around them, now a swirling, angry, mass of *bad*, ready to attack again, Shadrack said, *"Holly."*

A moment later, Holly Bear stepped into the circle of light, nodded to Shadrack and Wheely, pressed the gold button on her armband, thought two or three great positive thoughts, and started to shine brightly.

"Believer, Poppy, Scuba, Whisper, Theo, Marathon," Shadrack shouted out, signaling each of the waiting members of the Self-Esteem Team.

As he said their names, the bears of the Self-Esteem Team, the light of their individual auras transformed by their own attitude, each of them now great shining beings of light, stepped forward, their images gleaming and shimmering, like individual suns of intense light, gathered together in a galaxy of positive.

When the members of the Self-Esteem Team stepped forward in their suits of light, the *entire area* of Victoryland was bathed in beautiful, shimmering, positive light. It was like the heavens had come to Earth.

"Eli, are you here?" Shadrack said next.

"I am here, with you as always," the brightly gleaming light that was Eli said, suddenly standing next to Shadrack, creating a light that was as blinding as Shadrack himself.

"Let's let these Negatroids know the bears of Excellence are here!" Shadrack said.

And with that, the light in Victoryland became so bright that no Negatroid, no matter how evil or powerful, could create enough darkness to diminish it. It was the light of the combined spirits of the Incredibears of Excellence.

As the bears of Excellence lit up the world of Victoryland, a cheer went up from the children and their families who were there. What had been a nightmare of fear among them suddenly turned into a cheer of total excitement and joy.

This was *Victoryland*, and this must be a Victoryland show! As the children were cheering, seeing all of the incredible, amazing glowing, brilliantly lighted bears in front of them, they thought that this was a *performance*. It was all part of some special surprise entertainment, and the best show they had ever seen anywhere.

The Earth kids did not know that the future of their own lives, and the fate of planet Earth itself, was being played out in front of them. For the Negatroids who had surrounded them, and for the bears of Excellence who had come to defend the Earth kids, this was not a play at all. This was very real, and the future of all of planet Earth, not just the kids of Victoryland, depended on what happened next.

On the outer fringes of darkness around them, where the strongest of the Negatroids hovered, ready to attack again, an old, very evil Negatroid named "Vile," whose name was "evil," spelled in a different way, was getting his instructions from Low and No in the spaceship Neanderthal above him.

"Attack *now*," the Negatroid commander Low shrieked to Vile. "Attack now!"

"Attack the *light*," Vile commanded all of the Negatroid troops in Victoryland. *"Destroy the beings of light!"*

* * * * * * * * * * *

In the moment Shadrack saw the new attack was coming, he did not hesitate or waver.

"Why don't the Negatroids get it?" Shadrack asked himself. But out loud and clearly, Shadrack shouted the words *"Positron I, Positron II. Positron III, attend now!"*

While the outer dark rim of swirling Negatroids were preparing themselves to follow the Negatroid Vile's command to attack the beings of light, Shadrack's command summoned the giant robotic bears, the Positrons of Excellence, to enter the battle.

The first words that the kids in Victoryland heard, even before they saw what was coming next, were huge, powerful, words.

"GOOD . . . STRONG . . . POSITIVE . . . BELIEF," were the first thundering words they heard, as the giant bear Polaris, Positron I said, stepping into the light of the Self-Esteem Team, his steps shaking the ground as he walked. When he spoke, his clear, positive

words rumbled and echoed over Victoryland like a roar of thunder.

Turning slowly, the giant robotic bear, Polaris, held up one armband toward the mass of Negatroids that surrounded them, and paused for the next Positron to join him.

The ground shook again as Positron II, Ursus, entered the circle, booming out the words, *"POSITIVE WILL WIN. GOOD WILL ENDURE,"* and took his place, with a strong offensive stance, next to Positron I.

Then Positron III, Major, entered with thundering steps and a booming voice with the words, *"PEACE, LIGHT, LOVE and JOY,"* and the three giant Positrons, arms raised, together began to deflect the Negatroids' onslaught of negatives.

When the dark, swirling forms of the Negatroids, distracted now, turned to deal with the three giant Positrons, Shadrack and the entire Self-Esteem Team, side by side and all glowing brilliantly, charged the Negatroids.

With their suits of light shining brighter than they had ever been, and with their winning words of *positive* shouted out in unison, the Self-Esteem Team ran forward like they were charging toward the goal line in Great Bear Stadium. And no Negatroid was going to stand in their way.

With the brilliantly shimmering bears of light running full speed, straight at them, the swirling mass of Negatroids did the only thing they could do—they began to panic and break. This was too much for them. An unsuspecting Earth kid, here and there, was an easy target. But *this*? This was a defense of the kids of Earth that they had never *expected*.

And as *Negatroids* and *bullies* always think, when the chips are down, *"Run!"*

And that's exactly what they did.

* * * * * * * * * * *

In just minutes, with the Negatroids in full retreat, something wonderful began to happen.

One by one, the lights of Victoryland began to turn back on.

After their head-on charge into the center of the now fleeing Negatroids, Shadrack and the team regrouped, and turning toward the thousands of kids in the rides around them, Shadrack shouted, "Let's bring the fun back to Victoryland."

Then, looking exceedingly bright, he pointed a positive bear paw toward the giant double-wheel ride called the Skyrider, and focused all his positive light and energy forward. When he did, a beam of positive hit the huge ride filled with kids, and it began to turn once again.

Poppy, looking more like a swirling mass of sunlight than just a positive little bear, sent volumes of energy toward the "Earth-Shaker," and the great ride, filled with kids, started up again, slowly but surely gathered speed, and then shot forward, bouncing and churning, taking every rider aboard on an astounding journey into the depths of Earth, and the heights of space.

Scuba, whose bubble-like helmet even shimmered and glowed, sent an energy that totally lit up the submarine world of Whaleland, the popular underwater excursion in Victoryland.

One by one, each of the bears of Excellence, focusing their special positive light and energy, turned all of the lights and all of the rides in Victoryland back *on* again.

With all of the positives from the Self-Esteem Team, and with the Negatroids no longer draining the power and electricity out of Victoryland, one by one, every light and every ride turned back on. The Negatroids were fleeing, as fast as they could flee, and Victoryland was alive and running once again.

The last words Wheely shouted out, still shimmering and shining, and spinning in every possible direction in his little wheelchair were, *"When positive rules, Negatroids lose!"*

The usually brash, evil, bullying, and cowardly Negatroids were now receding to their armada of Negatroid starships to cower in the darkness of their defeat.

And as impossible as it might have seemed just a short time ago in Victoryland, *good* had defeated *bad*. *Positive* had *lived*. And the Negatroids, instead of being victorious, and destroying the children of Earth as they had planned, were fleeing, wheezing and screeching in confusion and dismay as they fled.

Chapter Nineteen

Negatroids in Defeat

Overhead, in the dark sky above planet Earth, the evil No and his brother Low were beside themselves in a frenzy of disbelief.

"When positive rules, Negatroids lose? All of our Negatroids are *retreating?* This can't happen!" the evil Low shrieked. "What are *bears* doing in Victoryland?" he screeched, falling backward over a stupid chair that shouldn't have been there in the first place. Trying to kick the useless chair in anger, he succeeded only in spiraling himself into an undignified spin, flailing in an ungainly way in midair.

Trying to stand upright, after the chair episode, he kind of caught his breath and wheezed, "There are no civilized bears on planet Earth! We left all of the positive thinking bears behind on Excellence," he croaked.

In his furor of disbelief and anger, the evil Low did the most amazing thing. He jumped up and down so angrily that he literally turned into what looked like a hornet's nest of hate and anger, a buzzing, wheezing frenzy of rage. *"Destroy every bear,"* he shrieked. "They can't do this! *Bears!*" he screamed, almost choking on the word. "They aren't even supposed to be on *Earth!*"

"Find their leader, and destroy him!" was the last thing the evil Low screeched before he lost himself entirely in an abyss of unrelenting darkness.

"Calm down," his equally evil brother No wheezed, knowing that trying to comfort a Negatroid was like trying to comfort a wasp when it was intent on stinging. "We will find their leader, the bear who did this to us, and we will destroy him."

"And exactly *who* will you find to *destroy?*" the evil Low coughed, coiling and churning, swirling in the air in agony, the early symptoms of the despair of defeat for Negatroids.

"Have *faith*, my brother," the evil No said, almost choking as he said the word "faith."

"I have watched the bears of Victoryland carefully. To defeat all of them, there is *one* bear we must destroy *first*," No said, thinking unusually clearly after the devastating defeat below them in Victoryland. "*We know the name of the bear who leads them.*

"His name is '*Shadrack*,'" No continued. "Defeat *that* one, and we will stop the bears and destroy planet Earth."

"But can we destroy him? Can we defeat something with so much positive power?" the dark, dejected Low asked.

"Oh, we *will*," the evil No said. "I assure you, before the sun sets on planet Earth tomorrow, we will have a plan to destroy the bear they call Shadrack," No coughed, trying to sound confident. "After all," he wheezed, hoarsely, "He's only a *bear!*"

* * * * * * * * * * *

Below them on planet Earth, in the last moments of the battle with the Negatroids in Victoryland, it was Shadrack who had had the final word.

"We will always defeat you," Shadrack shouted out to the fleeing Negatroids, who were scuttling and scurrying away in defeat. Each of them was trying to avoid the shimmering light of the members of Self Esteem Team who had saved the spirits of the children of Victoryland. *"Negative is always defeated by positive,"* Shadrack said.

Before he signaled his friends on the Self-Esteem Team, ready to return to *Earth Base I*, Shadrack paused, looking directly toward the evil Vile, the last of the remaining Negatroids to leave.

"Take this message home with you," Shadrack said. "You were not defeated by *physical force*; you were defeated by *positive belief*."

And then Shadrack said the words that caused the Negatroid to hide his evil head in dismay and chagrin.

"*But most of all*," Shadrack said, and then he smiled his Shadrack smile and tipped his head toward his best friend Wheely, "*You were defeated by a bear in a wheelchair.*"

* * * * * * * * * * *

Late that night, little Wheely Bear snuggled into his bed, thinking about the amazing day he had just gone through. He was almost asleep when he thought the word *"Excellence."* And then he thought the word *"Friends."* And then he thought the words, *"Running in a meadow."*

When he thought the words, he began to glow, very softly. And suddenly, with the glow, he felt as though he could actually *feel* his feet and toes, even though he had no real feeling in his feet or toes at all. "What if I could actually *walk* and *run?*" he thought.

As Wheely drifted off to sleep, with the soft, glowing aura of light still surrounding him, he saw himself running, on real feet and real legs, through a meadow of soft grass and sunlight. In his dreams, Wheely ran and played and had the *greatest,* strongest little bear legs and little bear feet that any bear had ever had.

As he dreamed, he smiled. And each time he smiled, his aura glowed a little brighter.

Chapter Twenty

Epilogue

While the bears of the Self-Esteem Team slept well in their safe quarters in *Earth Base I,* no one was asleep in the dark Negatroid command ship high above them in the night skies of planet Earth.

Hours after their defeat in Victoryland, the evil Negatroid No, and his equally evil brother Low, were still filled with anger and self-loathing. But the more tormented they became, the more intent they were on finding the leader of the bears who was responsible for their defeat.

"We will stop them!" Low said. "We will find their leader," he hissed, in a thin, hoarse whisper of a voice. "We will find this Shadrack Bear. We will take him someplace very special and very unexpected, . . . and then . . ." Low

breathed quietly, his voice trailing off, his eyes, thin slits of yellow green.

When he spoke again, there was an evil darkness in his voice. *"And then . . . we will take his spirit from him."* And then he added, in words with ice in them, *"And he will sleep in the coldness of the Nozone forever."*

The Negatroid ship *Neanderthal I* hovered through the night, surrounded by its armada of shadowy, ghost-like ships, waiting in the darkness. Far below the dark haze of Negatroid ships, the beautiful blue and white and green planet called Earth lay quietly in the heavens.

The people and the parents and the children of Earth could not know that if Shadrack and the bears of Excellence were stopped now, Earth's troubles would just be beginning. And planet Earth might never be the planet *Heart* ever again.

The End

Shadrack and the Self-Esteem Team
will return in

"The Rise of The Great Bear"

Listen to special self-talk for kids and adults from Dr. Shad Helmstetter

Self-Talk for Kids

Featuring Shadrack the Bear

Self-Talk for Older Kids

Self-Talk for Adults

Stream the top self-talk audio programs direct to your listening device.

www.SelfTalkPlus.com

www.SelfTalkPlus.com

For information:

Dr. Shad Helmstetter
www.shadhelmstetter.com

Self-Talk Audio Programs
www.SelfTalkPlus.com

Self-Talk Training
www.selftalkinstitute.com

Life Coach Training
www.lifecoachinstitute.com

Made in the USA
Columbia, SC
24 November 2024

47437656R00107